My Iowa Journey

SINGULAR LIVES:

THE IOWA SERIES IN

NORTH AMERICAN

AUTOBIOGRAPHY

ALBERT E. STONE,

SERIES EDITOR

My Iowa Journey

THE LIFE STORY OF
THE UNIVERSITY OF
IOWA'S FIRST AFRICAN
AMERICAN PROFESSOR

Philip G. Hubbard

FOREWORD BY ALBERT E. STONE

Ψ

University of Iowa Press

Iowa City

University of Iowa Press, Iowa City 52242

Printed in the United States of America
Design by Richard Hendel
http://www.uiowa.edu/~uipress

The publication of this book was
supported by the generous assistance
of the University of Iowa Foundation.
Printed on acid-free paper

Library of Congress
Cataloging-in-Publication Data
Hubbard, Philip G., 1921–
My Iowa journey: the life story of the University of
Iowa's first African American professor / by Philip
G. Hubbard; foreword by Albert E. Stone.
p.   cm.—(Singular lives)
Includes index.
ISBN 0-87745-672-0
1. Hubbard, Philip G., 1921–   . 2. University of
Iowa—Faculty Biography.   3. Afro-American
college administrators—Iowa—Iowa City
Biography.   4. College administrators—Iowa—
Iowa City Biography.   I. Title.   II. Series.
LD2567.H83A3   1999
378.1′2′0973—dc21
[B]   99-14788

99   00   01   02   03   C   5   4   3   2   1

TO ROSA BELLE WALLACE

My Guardian Angel

My Teacher

My Inspiration

My Mother

CONTENTS

Philip Hubbard's *My Iowa Journey* is the eighteenth volume in the University of Iowa Press' Singular Lives series. In this tenth anniversary of the series, it's perhaps appropriate to locate Hubbard in the literary-cultural context connecting the Singular Lives titles to other American success stories. Some are, like this one, written by older, educated, middle-class black men; one example is Cecil Reed's 1993 *Fly in the Buttermilk*. Others record the life experiences of women, Native Americans, immigrants, and other members of minority groups. The recent success (in print and on stage) of the Delany sisters' *Having Our Say* strikes a common note, as in a very different form does *Tight Spaces*, the immediate predecessor to *My Iowa Journey* in this series. Their accounts of black women reinforce the role of autobiography in educating and broadening American consciousness. Hubbard's contribution to this cause and the literature of the self bears a deceptively matter-of-fact subtitle: *The Life Story of the University of Iowa's First African American Professor*. This is doubly significant. First, it emphasizes memoir as the chosen mode of self-presentation. In Hubbard's case, a second choice has been to focus on his academic career and the University of Iowa as its locale. Probably the commonest of autobiographical choices, memoir records the experiences of a self (as both witness and actor) moving in the stream of history and society.

Thus this book captures the meaningful memories of a retired widower nearing eighty years of age who looks back on sixty years in Iowa City as an undergraduate, graduate student, professor, dean, and vice president. So a friendly but skeptical reader, one not intimately familiar with the campus, might well wonder if this writer can render interesting and important a somewhat conventional academic career spent at a single midwestern state university. It's a life story like few others but, on the surface anyway, less unusual than, say, the Delany sisters' "first hundred years" or W. E. B. Du Bois' final *Autobiography* with its even longer subtitle, *A Soliloquy on Viewing My Life from the Last Decade of Its First Century*. Hubbard has, I believe, met this challenge — not by direct emulation or contrast but by sticking to his own singular story. It proves to be a story of admirable personal commitment during an era of sweeping social change.

Hubbard's traditional title signals the first and major metaphor of self by means of which he has organized his story. As he shows, "journey" is an especially loaded term for African Americans. His Missouri forebears first imitated fellow slaves and exslaves by "following the North Star" over the border into free Iowa. There, in Des Moines, young Hubbard grew up hampered not only by family privation (they had no car, did a great deal of walking) but also by the racism that made even everyday travel difficult or impossible. Iowa, he found, was only a "half-open society." Even as a fly-in-the-buttermilk faculty family, the Hubbards for years had no car. A characteristic image is of the black vice president cycling around campus to his several duties — in the College of Engineering where he studied and taught, up the hill to Old Capitol, and across the Iowa River to the Museum of Art and Hancher Auditorium when he headed the Iowa Center for the Arts.

Also charged with racial overtones are Hubbard's accounts of family vacations in the Rockies. Once, en route, even a written reservation at a motel was abruptly canceled when the manager saw seven African American faces. As Hubbard's standing as a respected member of the Iowa Institute of Hydraulic Research grew, he lectured widely in the United States and abroad. Here another ironic destination was Mississippi. Where the younger engineer was once prevented from presenting a professional paper because of his race, years later he registered a victory by returning to Ole Miss to give its first engineering seminar.

This record of personal and family travel, always a challenge and often a closed door, is offered in Hubbard's typical low-key language. Aren't all serious scholars and university administrators great travelers? Not necessarily in the forties, fifties, or sixties. Readers may, in fact, be mildly shocked to learn that Hubbard's promotion and tenure came as late as 1956. "Journey" is everywhere linked to the central verities of Hubbard's life and character; race, family, education, career, church, and public service are all of a piece.

A second, equally historical metaphor of self by which Philip

Hubbard characterizes his mobile identity is turbulence. The noun first describes a professional preoccupation: measuring the turbulent movement of water in creeks and rivers. Public service and scientific research go hand in hand when accurately measured turbulence is applied to such practical problems as the undercutting of Iowa bridges, irrigation, and flooding. Erosion along the Mississippi River becomes a wider concern, as is air turbulence in airplanes or shock absorbers. So successful became this scientist that he founded his own businesses, the Hubbard Instrument Company and Hubbard Consultants (useful additions, he points out, to a modest salary).

Turbulence of another sort confronted Hubbard in the wake of the civil rights movement of the fifties and sixties. In Iowa, it took the shape of angry demonstrations by students and faculty mobilized to challenge the university. In the turbulent era of Vietnam, women's lib, and gay and lesbian rights, many felt surrounded by official complicity in an evil war and a corrupt society. Dean Hubbard had already spearheaded the university's adoption of sweeping new values. In loco parentis was ended as a rationale for housing and social regulations. Minority and women's representation was more actively pursued for both student body and faculty. A new code of human rights was enacted, with student participation. The university's official goals, during successive presidencies, were excellence, human rights, and affirmative action. Still ROTC remained, Dow Chemical recruited at the student union, and South Africa was a hotly debated issue — all leading to protest parades, broken windows, and threats of arson and mayhem. Hubbard's account of these tempestuous times strikes a tenuous balance between his (private) sympathy for the idealistic students and his (official) role as dean committed to keeping classrooms open to all and order on the campus. Here and subsequently, he's candid and apologetic in confessing his inexperience and his fears of radical change. Social turbulence, he discovered, could not be measured or always controlled like the floods of Iowa's rivers. Readers will gain some new, close-up insights into sixties and seventies America from *My Iowa Journey*.

A third essential feature of this honest historian may not strike the casual reader as an important metaphor of self to be added to travel and turbulence as unifying (and complicating) hallmarks of an evolving identity. However, the presence early and late of detailed lists of people whom Hubbard has known — and is indebted to — are true indexes of a consistent self. Even the demonstrators threatening the university's orderly operation include individuals whom the dean still lists as friend or mentor. Indeed, his steady rise to administrative eminence is at key points facilitated by "guardian angels," often white persons who took him under their wing. But this memoirist never forgets those beneath him in power and prestige who have known and supported him. Although the names and achievements of the six Iowa presidents he's known and served are here, so, too are the names (and often titles, families, and hometowns) of all his secretaries and assistants. After the death of his beloved wife, Wynonna, a scholarship is established in her name. Hubbard then identifies each of the first five recipients of the award. Gradually, the reader realizes that these individuals, high and low, black and white, are both themselves and representatives of human character, hard work, and achievement. They are, in addition, dimensions of Hubbard's self and serve to explain and verify his achievements.

Perhaps the final image of this friendly, dutiful autobiographer is contained in his account of his retirement. The recognition ceremonies involve the establishment of a small plot of land officially named Hubbard Park. Situated with more than casual care, these few acres stand near the east bank of the sometimes turbulent Iowa River. Across the river, upstream, lie the Museum of Art and Hancher Auditorium, parts of the Iowa Center for the Arts. Downstream stands the Institute of Hydraulic Research. Nearby is tiny Danforth Chapel, scene of marriages and memorials. A stone's throw up the hill is an intersection where angry demonstrators once tossed bottles at buildings. A few steps away is the Iowa Memorial Union. There, in the packed ballroom, the retiring vice president was feted by his many friends. However, Hubbard himself doesn't emphasize these personal associations. Instead, he remarks that Hubbard Park is only a short distance across Iowa Avenue from the Communication Studies Building, recently renamed in honor of longtime friend and colleague Sam Becker. Drawing attention away from single self but linking past and present, he reminds the reader that he and Sam Becker both entered the university as freshmen in 1940.

Students hurrying to class past Hubbard Park may not even know who's being honored there. Even fewer may be aware of the aptness of its location as a physical and symbolic space. But readers of this memoir can remember both. That is one of the uses of autobiography.

For many years, friends and colleagues have urged me to write my memoirs, and my recent completion of a book for the sesquicentennial celebration of the University of Iowa, *New Dawns: A 150-year Look at Human Rights at the University of Iowa*, raised some questions in my mind. What are my unspoken assumptions, values, and biases? In short, who is speaking in the book? Realizing that readers of that book and these memoirs might have similar questions, I sat before the keyboard that never knows which fingers will touch which keys, took mouse in hand, and proceeded to tell my story.

It begins in Macon, a county seat town in north-central Missouri, where its history as a former slave state dominated the relationship between the races. Segregation was the law, and its oppressive influence led indirectly to the departure of many African Americans to escape its stifling embrace. Since early in the nineteenth century, the state of Iowa has offered opportunity to those who wanted to escape the bonds and later the heritage of slavery. The underground railroad had a regular route through Iowa and Illinois or Wisconsin to Canada. African Americans in Missouri went to Iowa to enlist in the Union army and fight for their freedom during the Civil War, and Iowans offered hospitality and opportunity to George Washington Carver, a rejected native of Missouri whose work led to international recognition as a scientist. Mine is the story of the only remaining son of a Missouri family that moved its roots 140 miles to use the educational opportunities offered by the Hawkeye State. That initial emphasis on education guided my journey from elementary school through college, and eventually determined my career as professor, dean, and vice president of the University of Iowa.

In my judgment, my life has turned out rather well, but curiously enough, it is not a dream realized. Before it can be realized, a dream must exist, and the circumstances of my early life did not encourage great ambitions. Potential role models for a *career* were impossibly distant or had vanished before I could recognize them, although some of the people who remained were wonderful examples of healthy human relations. They were assets to be treasured and I am in their debt, but I was not conscious of any desire to emulate their careers. Even my namesake, Warren Gamaliel Harding, has been judged the worst of all presidents. Instead of pursuing a long-range goal, my journey has proceeded one step at a time, inspired by a wise mother, family encouragement, a determination to excel in each activity, and an expectation that achievement would lead to opportunity.

Some of the genealogical information that follows was collected at the Chicago office of the Bureau of the Census when my niece Paula Perkins Taylor took me there and helped with the search. An earlier draft was sent to my children and their spouses: Philip Jr. and Susan; Christine and James Walters; Michael Hubbard and Carol Torres; Richard Hubbard and Alaka Wali; and Peter and Mary. Their comments were very helpful and are incorporated into the chapters on the early years and family life.

I then consulted my daughter-in-law, Dr. Alaka Wali, an anthropologist and author with substantial experience in interviewing people for her research. In subsequent interviews over a period of several days, she probed my mind and revived memories that I had forgotten and some that I would not have been willing to include because they were painful or because others might not be interested. I am deeply grateful for her help.

Peggy Houston, director of the Iowa Elderhostel program, suggested that I take their course in memoir writing that was concurrent with the Summer Writing Festival in 1997. I followed her advice and appreciate the assistance of the instructor of the course, Cecile Goding, and her assistant Dalia Rosenfeld.

I

The Early Years

1

Life and Death Back Home

Our family origins are in the Bible Belt of small-town north-central Missouri, and my childhood was strongly influenced by an emphasis on religion, a work ethic, and a discriminatory restriction of opportunity. My family was of African ancestry except descendants of Mary "Molly" Guy, born in Clarence, Missouri, in 1863. Her mother was a freed slave, and she never knew her Irish father. Molly never went to school, and married Richard Milton Wallace (b. 1860 in Shelbyville), whose parents were also freed slaves. When they married, he was the huge, handsome, and unschooled section boss of a track crew (Gandy Dancers) on the Chicago Burlington and Quincy railroad. Their seven children were Alice (b. 1882), James (1884), Bess (1886), Rosa Belle (1888), Ben (1890), Mary (1892), and Bertha (1894). The last survivor was Mary, who died in Clinton, Iowa, at age 102.

Rosa Belle was a bright and beautiful girl who missed being a leap-year baby by one day; she was born on February 28, 1888. She finished high school and married Edward Wilbert Perkins, principal of Dumas public school (for African Americans) in Macon, the seat of next-door Macon County, twelve miles away. In the small community, strictly segregated by race, the high school principal was a community leader on a par with the ministers, and Edward was always called Professor Perkins. Their three sons were named Edward Jr. (b. 1909), Inman Laurence (1911), and Paul Milton (1915); Rosa Belle and Edward were admirers of Paul Laurence Dunbar, a well-known black poet who died in 1906, and named two of their sons for him.

Edward Sr. died when Paul was an infant. Rosa Belle then taught in one-room schools and eventually married Philip Alexander Hubbard of Macon, a craftsman. His father, John Henry Hubbard, and uncle, Philip Alexander Hubbard, had been ministers in African Methodist Episcopal churches in Missouri and Nebraska. My grandmother, Joanna Carter, was born in Missouri in 1847, and they lived in Hudson township (Omaha), Nebraska, when Philip was born in 1870. After her husband died, Joanna lived in Macon with her brother-in-law Philip and his first wife, Eliza. Edward (E. W., as we always called him), Inman, and Paul adored their stepfather (although the word stepfather was never used in our family; he was simply "Dad" or "Dad Hubbard"). In 1921, another brother joined them.

In attempting to trace my ancestry further back, I encountered the same problems that Alex Haley and my Iowa colleague Margaret Walker express so eloquently in their notable autobiographies. Genealogical information for slaves was kept with records of livestock or not recorded at all. I have not made a dedicated effort to follow up my family's genealogy, but my daughter-in-law, Alaka Wali, found a clue that might yield valuable information. A July 21, 1991, *Washington Post* article by Ken Ringle, "The Day Slavery Bowed to Conscience," reported the action 200 years earlier in which slave owner Robert Carter III of Nominee Hall, Virginia, freed 500 slaves as a private, nonpolitical act of conscience. Some of the freed slaves remained in Virginia, but many moved to other parts of the country, leaving few if any records of their whereabouts. The Deed of Manumission listed fifty-six names of freed slaves, including Hubbard. Some of the former slaves may have taken the name Carter, my maternal grandmother's surname. I have not pursued the clue further, but my descendants may choose to do so.

As Rosa Belle and Philip looked fondly at their bouncing ten-pound baby, they had no inkling that within the month

Rosa Belle would be widowed for the second time. The new arrival had been named Philip Gamaliel in recognition of the fact that I was born on March 4, the day that Warren Gamaliel Harding was inaugurated as president, but the boys wanted to know what my special name would be — their dad called them Big Bill, Middle Bill, and Little Bill. After a bit of thought he responded, "I guess we'll call him Bill Bill." They had scant opportunity to use the name, however, because Dad died of pneumonia eighteen days later, at age fifty-one. I was thereafter called Philip because our mother avoided the use of nicknames: in those days, white people regularly used diminutive names for Americans of African ancestry as a constant reminder that they were considered inferior. To avoid being completely ludicrous, they addressed senior citizens as Uncle or Auntie to circumvent the courtesy titles Mr. or Mrs. I heard an interesting example of the practice about Mary McLeod Bethune, noted educator and founder of Bethune-Cookman College in Florida. Pres. Franklin Roosevelt had appointed her as a special adviser on education, and arranged a reception in her honor. As the guests arrived at the White House, the doorman greeted them with "Good evening, Sir" or "Good evening, Ma'am." When the sixtyish and very dignified Bethune approached, the doorman greeted her, "Good Evening, Auntie." She looked at him closely and inquired, "Which of my brother's children are you?"

The shock of my father's death galvanized our family to gather its resources and assure Mother that she had allies for her ordeal as a young widow with four children. My older brothers were temporarily separated to live with relatives, and I was nurtured in Clarence by Grandma Molly and Grandpa Richard — the second in a continuing line of my guardian angels — while Mother taught school in small Missouri towns for four more years. I flourished under their experienced care; formal schooling is not essential to promote healthy physical growth. Their tiny home was separated from the railroad tracks by a dirt road, but its linoleum floor was always swept clean. A pump by the sink was the sole source of water, a porcelain bowl served as a washbowl, and an enameled chamberpot served as a "thunderstool." The generous yard was well maintained, and the large garden provided fruit and vegetables to go with the chickens and pigs, kept farther back. Uncle Ben, Aunt Letha,

Transplanted to Rich but Tainted Soil

Although he had never gone to school, Grandpa's many years as the respected no-nonsense boss of a crew of rough gandy dancers had endowed him with a rich vocabulary, much of which was seldom spoken on Sunday. When he worked in the house and yard and took me on walks, I watched and learned much about the way the world works. As Paul later told me, one day Mother overheard me quietly practicing a newly learned word: "sumbitch, sumbitch." She concluded that it was time to find another way to provide for her family.

Mother decided to sacrifice her teaching career in order to take advantage of the better educational opportunities for her four sons in Iowa's "unsegregated" schools (for students, not teachers; no African American teachers were hired). In 1925, she married William Washington Jones, whose family had moved from Richmond, Virginia, to Buxton, Iowa, in 1893 when he was twelve years old. He never entered school again, but "skinned" (that is, drove) the mules that hauled coal from the nearby mines. The now-defunct town of Buxton was created by the Consolidation Coal Company, which brought African American families from several areas in Virginia around 1890 to mine the coal in the Muchakinock mines southwest of Oskaloosa.

Buxton was planned as a model community with a wide variety of ethnic groups, but blacks predominated. Former black residents described it as "the Black man's Utopia in Iowa." Dad had worked as a field representative for the International Workers of the World labor union and as a chauffeur. He told me about the Winton automobile and removing the pistons as part of routine maintenance operations. He was grand secretary of the Prince Hall Masonic lodge in Des Moines and janitor in Frankel's clothing store when he and Rosa Belle married.

Because of the prohibition against African Americans as teachers, Mother worked as an elevator operator in Mandelbaum's department store and later as a freelance dressmaker. The birth of William Jr. in 1927 completed her family of five sons. Our baby-sitter during that period was elderly Mrs. Maywether, whom I remember as a mahogany-hued figure in a rocking chair, smoking a corncob pipe. The public schools of Des Moines provided the anticipated supplement to Mother's superb teaching skills, but she also provided oversight as an active member of the Nash Elementary School PTA.

Mother quickly corrected anyone who thought she was white because of her fair skin and auburn hair so long that she could sit on it, although she wore it in a bun. To her, they were reminders of an ancestor who was not man enough to acknowledge his own children, or as it was put colloquially, who neglected to leave a calling card. Although she never expressed hostility toward white people, her feelings were reflected in a distinct preference for people of strictly African ancestry, true of each of her three husbands. I thought that skin color was irrelevant and apparently my brothers felt the same way, even though we all married darker women.

She took pride in her appearance, and caught rainwater in a big barrel to be strained through silk hose before it was used to wash her hair, adding a little vinegar to the rinse water. I remember going to the store for Pond's cold cream and vanishing cream, wondering what the difference was between the two. When I was quite small, I overheard people saying that I was pretty, and finally I asked Mother, "Am I pretty?" She discouraged vanity by responding, "Pretty is as pretty does." I got the point. Her dresses were always made of yard goods selected by Dad, and I watched in fascination as she used patterns made of tissue paper, cut the material with pinking shears, and sewed the material into dresses on her treadle-operated Singer sewing machine. I sometimes used the machine to transform unbleached muslin into bags for marbles, but her scissors were never to be used to cut paper.

Music was one of Mother's favorite pastimes, and she often played the piano in our living room. William also played beautifully, but absolutely refused to do so in public, so that few people knew of his talent. Mother sang the aria "The Holy City" in the operetta *Heaven Bound*, and it has always been one of my fondest memories. The performance by local nonprofessional African Americans was produced around 1930 in the long-gone Princess Theater on 4th Street. One of the characters in the operetta was the devil, and I wish I could remember the name of the man who played the part and pranced around the auditorium in a red leotard with horns and a long barbed tail. Mother also sponsored the Lover's Club, an inspirational group for young African American women.

A family member recently asked whether Mother had "stepped down" in marrying a janitor with only an elementary school education after having married a high school principal and the son of a minister. I was taken aback by the question, because it had not occurred to me before. I didn't even know how an Iowan happened to be in Macon, but Dad's travels for the International Workers of the World carried him as far abroad as Oklahoma. Someone may have told him about the "Missouri Beauty" in Macon. He enjoyed reading newspapers and magazines, discussed current events intelligently, had achieved a high rank in the Masonic lodge, and led an honorable life in general, so his lack of formal education did not matter. We believed that manual labor was as honorable as mental labor, and that many well-educated people behaved dishonorably. I also realize that a widow with four young children was not in a favorable bargaining position, but Mother insisted that all of us retain our fathers' surnames and in other ways she retained control of our destiny.

Our sibling relationships were affected by the span of eighteen years between the oldest and youngest of my brothers. The nearest brothers to me were Paul, six years older than I, and William, six years younger. After William was born, Dad's violent outbursts finally caused E. W. and Inman to move away to escape his abuse. By then, I knew my brothers well enough to benefit from their strong affection and learned much about our earliest years "back home" from their conversations. Both E. W. and Inman were good students, and held jobs during and after high school, E. W. at the Paramount theater, and Inman first at a shoe shine stand in the Savery Hotel and then at the Des Moines theater, twin of the Paramount.

As the oldest brother, E. W. looked out for the rest of us but had no one in a position to help him, since Dad had effectively rejected him. Although he hoped to study dentistry, he was unable to get the support needed to go to college, and eventually he married Musette Jones of West Des Moines, a chubby and jolly woman who was one of my favorite people. Their pet names for each other were Ettesum (Musette) and Drawde (Edward). They had one daughter, Ardeth Jacqueline, with whom I baby-sat, and who we will hear more about later. Their divorce was a sad day in my life. E. W. moved to Vanport, Oregon, at one time, and established a successful dry-cleaning business. The flood of 1948 wiped it out, but he reestablished and expanded the business in Portland. After closing his business in Oregon, he moved back to Des Moines to be closer to relatives.

Inman worked for a while after graduating, then earned both bachelor's and master's degrees (1933 and 1938) in chemistry at the University of Iowa. Jobs were scarce when he graduated, but he found one teaching driver's education in a St. Louis high school and married a fellow teacher, Olivia Merriwether. They had no children, and he was drafted around 1941.

Paul and I did not play together very much because of the difference in our ages, but he was my constant advocate and defender when necessary. A "tubercular hip" (osteomyelitis?) interfered with his schoolwork, and he dropped out and went to work before finishing high school. Eventually he married Naomi Thurston and acquired a stepson, Maurice. Daughters Paula and Portia completed their family. After Naomi died of lupus, he married Corrinne Webster of Mason City. Paul was a maintenance man for the Meredith Publishing Company for many years until he retired, and the members of the New Hope United Methodist Church in Des Moines looked forward to his annual barbecue. So did we.

The six-year difference in age also meant that William and I had different circles of friends, but we got along well. Not always, however; he remembers that I sometimes teased him in a sneaky way, swatting him on the head and then innocently asking, "Why are you yelling?" I saw very little of him during his teens because I took an after-school job when he was ten years old and left for college when he was thirteen. He did not finish high school on schedule, but later completed a vocational program in linotype operation, a craft he did not pursue, primarily because he preferred to work independently. He spent many years performing janitorial services, bought and managed some apartments, and then purchased a one-man shoe repair business (Truman's) to finish out his career. At one time he served as president of a Des Moines Kiwanis club, and he adopted a disabled man in a Waterloo nursing home. He and Ida Mae Stewart became the parents of Jerome, Tyrone, Larry, Linda, and Rochelle Stewart but did not marry. After Dad died, William married Dad's widow Minnie and they lived in the family house until he died of diabetes in 1995. I have retained contact with Minnie and visit her and Paul's widow Corrinne when I am in Des Moines.

From the perspective of advanced years, I believe that my older brothers inspired me in ways I did not recognize. They always spoke of me in laudatory terms, protected me not only physically but also from information that they thought might give me pain, reveled in my achievements, and were distressed by my setbacks. I remember the tears in Paul's eyes and E. W.'s sadness when they saw me on crutches after suffering a ruptured Achilles' tendon at age fifty-three: I had a problem that they could not help solve. Their attitudes have carried on into the next generation, because Jackie and Paula are more like daughters than nieces. I have been pleased by their successes, and I am also glad that they derive vicarious pleasure from my successes, small and large. My brothers' families deserve the pleasure, because they were my early inspiration. Paul and E. W. each lived to age seventy-three.

Dad's personal life revolved almost exclusively around the Masonic lodge, and the only people ever invited to our home were Grand Master W. C. Buice and his wife. Buice was an oiler for the Northwestern Railroad, and I remember the big oilcan with a very long spout that he used to reach the inner portion of the engine mechanism. I also remember that they attended annual reunions of former Buxton residents even though they did not include members of our family other than Dad. His records as grand secretary for the lodge were written in green ink and kept in a drop-leaf desk that was always locked. The desk was in an extra room we called the library, where I spent many hours reading the modest collection Mother had brought from Missouri. I was impressed by the Masonic principle that forbade recruitment of new members. If one wanted to be a Mason, he had to apply and be screened for eligibility. I was not interested in joining because the lodge appeared to be primarily interested in the personal development of its members rather than bringing about changes in the general welfare.

Dad was a good example in honesty, hard work, management of money, and moderate personal habits — he smoked, but did not drink. I remember in particular his advice on interpersonal relationships: to criticize a man, tell him; to praise a man, tell others. Even his abusive conduct taught me a valuable lesson because I could contrast his actions with his professed beliefs; I have been especially responsive to requests for help to prevent domestic violence and abuse. In spite of his abuse of Mother and my older brothers, Dad was always kind to me. He knew that Mother would leave instantly if he started to abuse the last of her first four children. I appreciated his virtues and his consideration for me, but I could not accept his Dr. Jekyll and Mr. Hyde behavior, especially his verbal and physical abuse of Mother, the dearest person in my life. Thus, I treated him with reserved respect but not affection. After Mother's death, he was soon married again to his fifth wife, Minnie. Dad died of diabetes in 1962.

He did not interfere in Mother's disciplinary control over me, although he administered whippings on occasion, but Dad strongly opposed any attempts to discipline William. He finally decided that William's behavior was entirely contrary to his principles and general moral standards and he confronted him about the conduct of which he disapproved. The quick response was, "I didn't ask to be born: you brought me into this world and I am your responsibility." Whether because of that incident or because of an unsettled court judgment that would have consumed any property William might acquire, Dad willed all of his property to me with a life estate to Minnie as his surviving widow. The action surprised me; I was unaware of William's misdeeds when I was in the army and Dad had never indicated any intent to leave his property to me. I believed that William's children should have the house because they were Dad's only direct descendants, so after many years I deeded the property to William and Minnie, who had shared the house for thirty years.

Our neighbors across the street, Theodore and Virginia Martin, had also migrated from Missouri, where Virginia's father had been bishop of the AME Church. She was Mother's closest friend, and we saw them often; their nearness may have been a factor in the selection of our home. The Martins owned an automobile that only Virginia could drive, and I remember that they once invited us to accompany them on a short trip to Ledges State Park.

In addition to our family, almost all of Mother's siblings followed the North Star to Iowa. Alice, James, Bess, Mary, and Bertha all moved to Clinton, attracted by the railroad construction under way following World War I. James worked on a construction crew, while Bess and Mary cooked in the Northwestern depot restaurant. Only Ben remained in Clarence. When Grandpa died of apoplexy in 1927, Grandma moved to Clinton and lived with Bess and Mary until she died in 1940. I especially remember Alice's son Ralph Holder, a great cigar-chewing bear of a man who once played professional football as a running guard with the Chicago Brown Bombers. During Prohibition, he operated a speakeasy in a house near the Mississippi River on 2nd Avenue North in Clinton. Mary and Bertha married members of a Dixieland jazz band in Clinton that later moved to Omaha. Bertha's husband, Frank Perkins, was the leader of the band, known as Red Perkins and his Dixie Ramblers, and Mary's husband, Eugene Freels, was the lead trumpet player. I especially liked their renditions of music by Scott Joplin and Duke Ellington. The band played in many places in Missouri, Nebraska, and Iowa, including the Billiken Club in Des Moines. Frank was also from Buxton, where his father had owned substantial property. He and Dad were among many African Americans who moved to various places in Iowa when the mines were abandoned after World War I.

Mother's siblings had interesting names for one another: Alice was always "Sis," and the nieces and nephews called her "Aunt Sis"; James was called "Bounce" or Uncle Bounce; Bess was known as "Cumps" (but Aunt Bess); Mary was called "Dumps" (but Aunt Mary), and Bertha's nickname was "Bert." Aunt Mary was a staunch Republican, and came to Des Moines as an assistant to Clinton County representative Lawrence Carstensen whenever the legislature was in session. When Mary visited Des Moines she stayed with Victoria Cogswell, who I believe had also migrated from Missouri.

Mother prepared me very well for school, and I eagerly looked forward to the experience. I adored my kindergarten teacher, Miss Gode (we knew most teachers only by their last names), even though she rapped my wrist for an offense I remember only because Mother punished me again when I got home. Thanks to her influence, reading was a favorite pastime, and I became very familiar with the downtown library. Greek mythology and books by James Fenimore Cooper, Rudyard Kipling, and Nathaniel Hawthorne were among my favorites.

Our small library at home included the Junior Classics, and I read all ten volumes over and over again. Most of my reading was accomplished while sitting in a little rocker that I must have outgrown when I was still in elementary school. When I wanted to find the meaning of a word, I went to the nearby unabridged *Webster's* dictionary. A lexicographer might have been pleased to see me trying to use that tome; it was always an interesting experience because I became diverted into reading it page to page as if it was a storybook. The book introduced the cast, and I supplied the plot, learning the meaning of strange words in the bargain.

I would probably have received an excellent education from Mother at least through eighth grade without enrolling in the public schools. My parents avoided any discussion of sex, but one day when I looked through the bookcase, I found a book I had not seen before, with the title *Vivilore*. It described the human body, and was my first opportunity to learn about female anatomy. I now suspect that the placement of the book when I was at the "right" age was Mother's attempt at sex education.

Classes began twice each year, with those starting in the fall designated 1A, 2A, and so forth, and those starting in February designated 1B, 2B, and the rest. This meant that all of the students in a particular class were within a six-month age range, and class sizes were small enough so that each of us knew all the others. I can still remember almost all of their names, from Bernard Arenson, whose father owned the grocery store next to the school, to Edna Zarafis, one of three Greek American students in the class. I thought that Janet Roth was the prettiest girl in the class, August Gruening was a wizard in woodworking, and Stanley Little was a BIG MAN ON CAMPUS. Wayne Allen and I were born on the same day, and his handwriting was exceptionally good in contrast to mine. Bertha Rothman was an excellent student, and our music teacher in junior high, Hoyt Irwin, became quite excited when he thought that she had perfect pitch. Our gym teacher, "Hoffie" Hafenstein, was a small, wiry man who insisted that we drop our baseball bats on a mat while running to first base in the gym. The assistant principal, C. O. "Dad" Hoyt, was a very large and well-liked man who was responsible for student discipline, and he later became assistant superintendent of the Des Moines schools.

My grades were always good, and I would have had to answer to my mother if she felt that I was not making a full effort. She believed, as I still do, that I should not be concerned about grades relative to classmates; our standard of comparison was my own best effort. Reflecting her experience as a teacher, she informed me in no uncertain terms that if the teacher punished me for misconduct, I could expect more punishment when I came home. She had studied Latin and taught me some of the rudiments of Latin grammar and the Latin name for all the bones and parts of the human body. Her teaching, support, and encouragement were primarily responsible for my early start in reading and in winning the spelling championship in Nash Elementary School as a sixth-grader in 1933. I still remember the word I failed to spell correctly in the city-level competition — "supersede." Many years later, I attended a lecture at the University of Iowa and met the coauthor of the Horn-Ashbaugh speller we used at school. Ernest Horn was ninety-five years old at that time, and discussed the characteristics of the English language that made spelling so difficult in comparison with Spanish, for example. When he referred to the absence of any pattern in the spelling of suffixes in words such as recede, succeed, and supersede, I said "Amen!"

Although I joined the Iwakta Club (biology) and played freshman football, my principal activities in Washington Irving Junior High and North Senior High were musical — band, orchestra, glee club. Following in my father's footsteps, I played baritone horn in both band and orchestra, using the bassoon score for orchestra since there was usually no part for the baritone and no player for the bassoon. I played in the all-city high school band in summer 1938, which enabled me, for the first time, to sit in the grandstand at the Iowa State Fair. Although I had often attended the fair on children's day, my fifty-cent allocation had been inadequate to gain admission to the grandstand or other events requiring money. We played Ravel's "Bolero," thereby fulfilling my teacher's wish to have a band large enough and competent enough to play it. I also remember playing in the marching band at football games when the weather was so cold that I had to put the mouthpiece of the horn in an inner pocket to keep it from freezing to my lips when I played.

Music also led to my very first trip to Iowa City and the university in 1938. We could not afford private horn lessons, but diligent practice was the key to success. To avoid disturbing the neighbors when practicing at home, I removed the bell from the horn and put a cloth over the resulting wound. The horn thus produced only a mournful cry during the many hours of practice, but sang for joy when its beloved crown was restored. I won the solo competition on the baritone horn (a nice shiny one, not the battered one inherited from my father) at the city level and at the regional level in Guthrie Center, the home of my friend and longtime director of the university orchestra, James Dixon. I then advanced to the final competition in Iowa City (my first visit to the university campus). My selection, "The Southern Cross," was originally composed for cornet or trumpet, and begins with a delightful cadenza in which the quality of the sound is much more important than technique. My accompanist for all of the competition was Benjamin Dacus, a classmate at North High.

I have primarily pleasant recollections of the Des Moines school years; one might say that the schools were in the open part of a half-open society, and they opened the doors of opportunity that Mother had sought when we moved north to Iowa. Macon plus 140 miles by train equals Des Moines; tradition plus 140 miles equaled opportunity. However, opportunity for minorities was an option to be discovered only by individual initiative, not an alternative promoted by school representatives. When I attended the celebration of North High's seventy-fifth anniversary, I met my old principal, S. E. Thompson, who was visibly surprised to learn that an alumnus he never heard of was a professor and dean at the state university. Nearly fifty years after graduation, I was elected to the North High Alumni Hall of Fame after being nominated by Dean Woodford, a former classmate.

Fifty-five years after we graduated from high school, I heard from Patricia Woods, who had joined our class in the second grade and who I remember very well as one of my liveliest and brightest classmates. An Iowa City friend of her family knew that we had gone to school together and sent her a newspaper clipping about my retirement. When she visited Iowa City from her home in California, we had lunch together and reminisced about old times (what else?). We had been out of touch for fifty-two years, were both without a spouse, and I wish she lived closer to Iowa City. More recently, Ethel Rowe called me while her husband was in the hospital, and she brought me up to date on some of our classmates from more than a half century ago.

Although my family and I were not particularly well known in Des Moines before I left for college, I have been invited back on many occasions to speak in high schools and at African American churches and community centers as a hometown boy and a representative of the University of Iowa. I have been pleased to accept, because the people of the community contributed to my growth and I want to pass it on. My visits were not limited to Des Moines, however; I have made repeated student recruiting trips to every city in Iowa with a significant minority population and to some towns without any known minorities.

Religious beliefs continued as a major influence during my childhood; alcoholic beverages, card playing, dancing, gambling, and profanity were taboo, except that Dad ignored the latter when his brooding temper flared into violence. I have continued to avoid profanity, not for religious or aesthetic reasons, but I noticed that some of my friends were almost inarticulate in situations where they couldn't use a cussword. The same expletive served as a verb, noun, adjective, or adverb, according to the context.

A typical schedule for Sundays was St. Paul AME Sunday school followed by church services, then home for dinner. Mr. Gould, the Sunday school superintendent, and Mrs. Warrick, the elementary school supervisor (I never heard their first names), ruled with firm but loving hands. The leader of the upper division was S. Joe Brown, a graduate of the University of Iowa Law School in 1901 and a splendid role model for young and old. He was known as a poverty lawyer because his fees were relatively low and he readily represented low-income clients. The church organist was Joburness Kelso, who also produced the operetta *Two Haunting Eyes* with teenage performers at the local community center; I still remember the songs from that production even though I played second fiddle to Willy Clinton in the starring tenor role.

After dinner we attended a program at the Crocker Street branch (that is, the segregated branch) of the YMCA where the director, Quentin Mease, provided capable oversight. Dad was a Baptist, but refused to go to church because he disapproved of the minister's personal behavior. He was a regular participant at the YMCA program, however, and we enjoyed singing songs such as "Let the Lower Lights Be Burning" a thousand miles from the nearest ocean. Aside from a few books in our home library about Booker T. Washington and other notable pioneers, those meetings were my only opportunity to learn about the history of African Americans — the only references in school related to their role in the Civil War. Occasionally we would go to services at the Blue Triangle YWCA (another segregated branch), where Sue Brown was a prominent figure. I remember a notable program featuring Mary McLeod Bethune, an inspirational leader in higher education for whom Bethune-Cookman College in Florida was named. Evening activities included Christian Endeavor (the AME youth fellowship), then occasionally going to the Baptist Young People's Union at Corinthian Baptist Church to fill out the evening. The baptismal font intrigued me because immersion was not used in the Methodist

Church. Occasionally, I attended Baptist worship services, and enjoyed the swinging music style of the organist, who was the wife of Rev. George Robinson. Their son George sang in an excellent male quartet with robust voices and a strong bass that made most barbershop quartets sound thin and pale in comparison.

Each member of the family had responsibilities for maintaining the house and yard, and the absence of sisters (sex-role stereotypes were common) meant that I had many household chores. Washing dishes, vacuuming, and some cooking were part of my work in addition to tending the smoky furnace, maintaining the yard and the flower garden, and sweeping the sidewalk before going to school (brooms wore out very quickly). I dreaded spring cleaning — the floor registers had to be cleaned, and clearing the closet under the stairs revealed lost items. The soft coal we burned in the furnace produced huge clinkers that were hard to separate from the grates, and produced soot and dust that coated the wallpaper. In the spring, I cleaned the walls by rubbing them with a baseball-size wad of pink claylike substance that quickly turned black.

I cultivated Dad's garden with its many varieties of flowers; the only edibles in the garden were vines bearing Concord grapes. Except for special occasions, my only source of cash was income from chopping wood and running errands for neighbors. That income was measured in pennies, but one cent was enough to buy a little wooden cupful of peanuts or "red hots" at Shreck's corner store near school. As a teenager, I tried to sell magazine subscriptions and Earl May seeds door to door, and learned that my salesmanship skills were very poor; I have always preferred teaching someone who wants to learn rather than trying to convince people to do something.

Plenty of time was left for outdoor play with neighborhood friends. Charles (five days younger than I), Joe (born on the same date as my future wife Wynonna), and Lawrence Howard, sons of a prominent lawyer; Adam and Lacie May Johnson, whose father was a barber in a shop of black barbers that served only white customers; Charles Johnson, who graduated with me from North High in the spring of 1939, and his sisters Haleyozeal, Vegasalonica, and Thyravalee; Jim McGuire, the son of the only black police detective in Des Moines; and Edward and

Edwin Patten, twin sons of a printer whose work was featured in the fall 1996 issue of *Iowa Heritage Illustrated*. Lack of money meant that our activities were restricted to games that required little or no equipment or special facilities — races around the block, "hot butter and blue beans," in which the finder of a hidden switch used it to whip anyone he could catch before they reached a safety zone, and skating on the streets after a winter ice storm, for example. I also remember watching the flow of melted snow in the spring as it cascaded down a slope and dropping a twig into the water flowing into a tunnel through the ice, then seeing it emerge at the other end. A baseball had to be kept in service by frequent applications of tape, and worn-out roller skates were salvaged and converted into homemade scooters. I spent many hours running behind the rim of a worn-out wagon wheel, pushing it with a "T" made of two sticks.

Organized team sports involving parents, such as Little League, were unheard-of; in fact, I never played games of any type with Dad. Charles and Joe Howard joined the Boy Scouts, but Dad refused to let me join because he did not trust the two single brothers who served as scoutmasters. We spent a lot of time at Good Park on 17th Street, and I remember the agony of crossing Keosaqua Way at midafternoon in August with bare feet on bricks hot enough to fry eggs, followed by the welcome feel of the cool grass in the park. We welcomed the construction of a swimming pool at the park, and I surprised the bigger boys by my unexpected skill at water polo. I also remember wondering if I would live until my seventy-ninth birthday at the dawn of the twenty-first century.

A high point of some years was attendance at the Des Moines "Y Camp" at Boone. African American boys were relegated to the very last "special" period of the summer, and the fee for that week was only $5, thanks to a subsidy from a Des Moines service club. Henry Hasbrouck and Howard Crawford from the central YMCA in Des Moines oversaw the operations, but most of the regular operating staff was sent home for the year. Only a couple of the usual crafts were available, and African American operating staff and cooks were brought from Des Moines. We always looked forward to the meals prepared under the supervision of A. A. Trotter, who operated a restaurant on Center Street. At the evening campfires, the leaders recited "The

Cremation of Sam McGee" and other spine-tingling tales. Although in 1929 I was below the minimum age for attendance, an exception was made for me because my fourteen-year-old brother Paul could look after me, just as he and my other brothers always did. He watched me with special care when we swam in the Raccoon River in those early years, before a nice swimming pool was built.

I especially remember the inspirational songs:

> One nine two nine at our Y Camp
> No other year the same
> Every boy a comrade true
> Whatever school or fame.
> One nine two nine at our Y camp
> Sunset and evening glow
> But it's the inspiration most
> That makes us love you so.

Another song, which had a lasting influence, was:

> Dear Old Y camp, dear old Y Camp
> Our love for you is great
> You put within our hearts this day,
> Respect for God and state
> You also teach us how to live
> As real boys ought to live
> With cheerfulness and kindness
> And less of take than give
> We are the boys of the Y Camp of Des Moines
> Standing for the right 'gainst wrong
> Building bodies that are strong
> Big men, strong men, that's what we shall be
> If you don't believe it, just watch a bit
> For we're the boys of the Y camp, the Y camp
>   of Des Moines.

I now realize that my sensitivity to discriminatory influences must have been quite selective. The "Y" excluded us from its facilities and services for white people, yet I accepted its inspirational principles as applicable to me. Similarly, when I read in the Declaration of Independence that "all men are created equal," I thought I was included, even though the framers of the declaration intended "all property-owning white males are created equal." Ah, the blessed innocence of youth!

Around 1933, a sports announcer for radio station WHO in Des Moines heard about the "Y camp boys," and invited several of us from the "special" period to sing camp songs on his radio show. Little did anyone suspect that the announcer, Ronald "Dutch" Reagan, would eventually be elected president of the United States.

Around 1929, the Wynn family around the corner on 14th Street bought the first radio in our neighborhood, and I went to see the marvelous device that was so much better than the crystal set I had seen. Later, another pleasure was listening to radio broadcasts of prizefights when Joe Louis was at his prime. We suffered agony when he was knocked out by Max Schmeling, and cheered when Louis made short work of Schmeling in a rematch. Amateur boxing matches were also staged on Wednesday evenings in an outdoor ring at the Crocker Street branch of the YMCA. I attended the Drake Relays a few times, and followed the achievements of such great sprinters as Ralph Metcalf, Eddie Tolan, and Jesse Owens.

It would be hard to overestimate the exultation in the black community in seeing the response of Hitler to the victories of Louis and Owens in the Olympics. They carried our colors into the ring and onto the track. They didn't need the nod of the emperor to validate their superiority, and they flaunted the oppressor before the world; they had wounded the dragon.

I have lost contact with most of my childhood friends, but I know that Adam Johnson joined the U.S. Marines. I last saw him at the Minneapolis airport where he had a job delivering luggage; he died in a traffic accident after returning to Des Moines. I once had a crush on his sister, Lacie May, who joined the Women's Army Corps, returned to Des Moines, and eventually died in a murder/suicide by her husband Calvin Dacus, brother of Benjamin, my accompanist in high school. Charles Howard graduated from Drake Law School, established a life-long practice in Baltimore, and became president of the National Bar Association. His father had been a founding member of the association, which was created because African Americans were not admitted to the American Bar Association. Joe Howard attended the University of Iowa, graduated from Drake

Law School, practiced in Baltimore, and spent many years as a senior judge in the Fifth Circuit Court, District of Maryland. The youngest Howard brother, Lawrence, graduated from Drake University, earned a master's at Wayne State and a Ph.D. at Harvard, and eventually served as professor and dean of the Graduate School of Public and International Affairs at the University of Pittsburgh.

Another North High classmate, Charles C. Johnson Jr., received bachelor's and master's degrees in engineering from Purdue University, then served as assistant surgeon general in the U.S. Public Health Service, associate executive director of the American Public Health Association, vice president of the Washington Technical Institute, president of C. C. Johnson and Malhotra, P.C., and retired in 1994 as executive director of the Water for People Foundation (American Water Works Association). His alma mater recognized his achievements in 1995 with an honorary doctorate in engineering.

When I say that I once had a crush on Lacie May, I recall the limitations of living in a socially segregated community where African Americans were a very small minority (around 4 percent). The number of "eligible" girls was very small, and they were spread over a considerable distance. Add to this the limitation of having to walk everywhere, and the nearest girl begins to look pretty good. Lacie May's personality was quite the opposite of mine: she liked slick boys who were good dancers, and I had two left feet. She liked snappy dressers, and I placed very little emphasis on clothes. Her tastes in music and recreational activities were distinctly different from mine, and we really had very little in common. In retrospect, she seems to have been destined for a tragic fate. At a certain age, however, one tends to wear rose-colored glasses when looking at the few eligible choices.

Somehow, I don't seem to remember the irksome events of my childhood as clearly as I do the pleasures. That may be because of our family's generally good health; our illnesses were temporary and did not require hospitalization. Another explanation may be that large problems tend to overshadow small ones, and we had enough problems to keep us too busy to fret about little frustrations. The one event that remains in my mind is ridiculously petty, but the memory has carried through into my postretirement years. Dad's job in a clothing store kept him informed of current fashions, and he seemed to like knickers, or "plus fours," so he bought a pair for me to wear to school. They were okay for warm-weather wear, but the exposed ankles became a problem in the winter when I had to wear long underwear, which I hated. (I always caught a cold when I switched back to BVDs in the spring.) Try as I might, I could not fold the long underwear over my ankles without making a bulge that I imagined was so blatantly obvious that I might as well have worn bells on my ankles. I now realize that others probably didn't even notice, but childhood sensitivities are hard to explain.

Our family and many others without automobiles depended on public transportation for errands beyond walking distance, so small neighborhood stores were a hallmark of the community. Within a five-block radius of our house were five corner groceries, a one-man drugstore whose proprietor once shot dead a would-be robber, an ice house, an ice-cream parlor, and a larger grocery on Keo Way. Jews owned most of these small businesses, and some of them also served as the home of the owners. In general, our relations with the Jewish community were quite friendly, and we would often stop at the Jewish Community Center to shoot baskets in their gym on the way home from high school. I seemed to have an especially warm relationship with the Jewish students in my classes. Dad often referred to the wisdom of Rabbi Eugene Mannheimer, but I don't remember the context except that it was admiring. Although their businesses were nearby, Jewish families with children lived outside of our immediate neighborhood so that I saw my Jewish friends only at school. Only two white children lived on our street in the early years: Nina Howard and Walter Torgerson. Nina's only contact with our family came when she was tracing a rumor that she was adopted, and she asked Mother whether she knew. Walter lived with his widowed grandmother, and was a regular playmate.

Street vendors and home delivery services were quite common because many people did not have cars and the wives were usually at home during the day. Milk was delivered to homes daily, and I remember the chimney of frozen cream that crept from the milk bottle as it sat on the open porch in subzero weather. The wagon from Flynn Dairy was pulled by a team of horses that were well known for their knowledge of the delivery route, stopping at each customer's house while the driver took milk to the porch, and moving independently to the next house. Mother always took her scissors to be sharpened by the grinder who came by occasionally, bought vanilla and other flavorings from the Watkins man who sold door to door, and bought catfish, carp, and bullheads from street vendors who had brought them directly from the Des Moines River. The life insurance salesman came by weekly to collect the fifteen-cent premiums for the policy on each family member.

Much of the pre–World War II social and commercial life of the west side African American community was on or near Center Street, along the half-mile strip from Keosauqua Way to 17th Street. Businesses included Mitchell's drugstore, the Billiken Club, the Sepia Club, Hardaway's barbershop, Watkins Hotel, La Marguerita Hotel, Patten's Printing Shop, Trotter's Restaurant, and some other restaurants. The Community Center at 17th Street marked the west end of the district in the thirties, when I lived there. Keosauqua Way separated the commercial district from St. Paul's AME Church and the Crocker Street branch of the YMCA. The entire area was dislocated in 1958 by reallocation of land associated with construction of freeway I-235 in a manner that has become familiar throughout the nation.

The Harlem Renaissance was in full bloom during my childhood, but I cannot recall that its rich literature had any effect on our community. Our performing arts culture, especially music, seems to have risen from Chicago, St. Louis, New Orleans, and other southern cities more than from the East Coast, except for the Virginia influence in the coal-mining areas. As African Americans from the states bordering the lower Mississippi River followed the North Star to Iowa, their talents and traditions formed the basis of the culture in their relocated communities.

Racial customs in Des Moines were remarkably bipolar. Because our home was just outside the boundary of the "black" area at that time, I was usually the only nonwhite child in my classes and was accepted on an equal basis; outside of school, the races were separate and highly unequal. Although legal segregation and enforced barriers were less common in Iowa than in some parts of the country, the everyday rebuffs and indignities we suffered created an atmosphere of wary skepticism regarding contacts with the white community. For example, I learned to swim in the pool in the "white" YMCA downtown, but we could use it only in the late afternoon on Saturdays, just before the pool closed for cleaning over the weekend. When we attended the movies, we were directed to the balcony. Many restaurants would not serve us except for carryout orders; they wanted our money but not our presence. Apparently many of the discriminatory practices were not supported by statutes, but were inflicted at the whim of an individual owner or group of businesses; the victim had no legal recourse. I was distressed by evidence that many African Americans, including some nationally prominent role models, had internalized the negative image projected by racists, leading them to use skin whiteners, caustic hair-straightening compounds, and deferential behavior toward white people, for example. My attitude could best be expressed by the motto of a later generation, "Black is Beautiful," and my belief that people should be comfortable with their natural heritage.

Perhaps the most damaging discrimination was in employment, where opportunities for African Americans were severely limited: no firefighters, one deputy sheriff, only a handful of police officers in primarily black neighborhoods, one bailiff and one secretary in the court system — virtually no blacks were employed by white businesses except as janitors. A slaughterhouse on the south side employed a large number of African Americans, including Dad's father at one time. Many of the employees lived nearby, and the smell in the neighborhood was so bad that we could detect it several miles away, across the business district, on the opposite side of town when the wind shifted to the southeast.

When I returned for summer vacation after enrolling in college, I applied for a temporary job at the city waterworks that employed some students. In spite of my major in engineering and my employment at the Iowa Institute of Hydraulic Research, I was rebuffed with "Sorry, you're the wrong color."

That summer was not a complete loss, however: I got a job at the Holland Dutch bakery on Ingersoll Avenue driving a delivery truck to the retail store downtown. First, I had to learn to drive — my first license was as a chauffeur driving a rickety panel truck, the only vehicle at my disposal.

Lynching had been a common practice in the South, and the trial of the "Scottsboro boys" occurred when I was ten years old. The shadow of oppression was sometimes reflected by our playful boyish banter. For example, what is the most dangerous animal in the world? A man-eating tiger, an enraged buffalo, a cobra? No, none of those. The answer is: a white woman — she can destroy a black man by merely pointing a finger and uttering one word, "rape."

In general, my family lived happily in the sunlight of our African American society, and I was not preoccupied with the indignities inflicted on us because of our race. Instead, I believed that the perpetrators of oppression were debasing themselves by acting contrary to their professed religious and political values. Furthermore, if I failed to develop my innate potential because of a preoccupation with the unfairness of our treatment, then the would-be oppressors would have achieved their goal. I have never permitted *anyone* to define who I am; that is my privilege and my obligation, and I have *never* perceived myself as being downtrodden or deprived of assets essential to my quality as a human being. After all, I studied and played with white children at school and knew many people in the African American community, and saw no reason to believe that either race was inherently superior or inferior. The refusal to be intimidated or stereotyped served as an antitoxin against racism, and although I denounced discriminatory acts, I could not blame white people categorically because, on the whole, acts of kindness far outnumbered insults. My experience at an early age, reinforced throughout my life, taught me that the attitude of a person cannot be predicted by the color of his or her skin; the colors of the helping hands extended to me have been like a rainbow of the human family. With that background, I went about preparing for future opportunity.

What have I learned from my experience as a minority in a nation based on the immediately ignored premise that all men are created equal? During the first third of my life, I tended to view racism as an essentially American phenomenon, the legacy of slavery: white versus black, with "one drop of African blood" being enough to place someone in the suppressed group. As my perspective widened and I viewed events elsewhere in the world, I realized that race is merely one of an endless number of categories used to divide people in the "might is right" competition, primarily economic, for the things people most desire — material wealth, land, sensual pleasures, and power over others. Although perpetrators of racism may have a primarily economic motivation, they are readily supported by a coalition of sociopaths and people of low self-esteem whose actions are based on hatred and fear.

Slavery in ancient Rome was not based on skin color, nor was the Indian caste system. Contemporary adversaries in Europe, Africa, and the Middle East appear from a distance to be racially indistinguishable: the "tribe," usually defined by language or religion, is often the most important basis for identifying friend and foe. Even within a homogeneous population, "royal blood" of divine origin has long been the basis for a claim of superiority from generation to generation. Although "blood" has traditionally been cited as the decisive inherited factor in racism, the increasing use of genetic tracing may shatter many illusions. It is unlikely, however, that rational considerations will solve the problem of racism or tribalism because people cannot be reasoned away from prejudices that they were not reasoned into. Those with economic and political advantages will never cease to divide and conquer in ways that will preserve their advantage, so that eternal vigilance is the cost of freedom from racism, sexism, anti-Semitism, and other dogmatic "isms."

These comments are not to be perceived as a defense of American racism, because that is an abomination that should be denounced. My point is that a problem cannot be approached effectively unless its true character is recognized; a strategy for protection from a wildcat may be inadequate to deal with a polecat. The oversimplification of black versus white is only one example of a strategy of divide and conquer, and the many groups who are victims of unfair and unreasonable exploitation should recognize their common interest in resisting the corrosive influence of "isms."

This analysis may sound pessimistic and bode ill for a solution to "America's peculiar institution" (Gunnar Myrdal) or "the problem of the 20th century" (W. E. B. Du Bois), but I am stubbornly optimistic. The large portion of the population who see humans as a single family will provide the vaccine to prevent racism and tribalism from destroying civilization. I believe that the actions of many people described in this book provide substantial evidence to support this statement.

Many people remember the economic depression of the 1930s as a time when fortunes were lost overnight, stockbrokers jumped from high buildings, joblessness was a blight on practically every community, and bread and soup lines were set up to prevent general starvation. It was indeed a period of great stress, but some people near the lower end of the economic ladder who already relied exclusively on their daily labor felt much less of a shock. Almost all the people in my neighborhood were janitors or other unskilled laborers; a barber and a police detective were among the most affluent until a lawyer and a dentist moved into houses whose owners could no longer afford the properties. Menial labor was still in demand even in a depression, and those who were in good health and willing to do such work could manage to survive by working long hours seven days a week. The Great Depression thus served as an equalizer of living standards because those near the bottom had very little room to fall.

My family was fortunate in this regard because we were familiar with menial labor and already were living frugally; the equity in our Des Moines home at 1318 Ascension Street was our only capital asset. The inherited "home place" in Macon had been free of debt, but was lost because we were unable to collect rent to pay the taxes. Many goods were purchased on "layaway" installment plans. One of Dad's proudest achievements was his perfect "25-p" (p for prompt) credit rating. When he was unable to pay a mortgage installment or other debt in full at the due date, he always paid what he could and asked for an extension, which was readily granted. We never owned or had access to an automobile, so that walking everywhere was the norm. Curiously, a result was that I learned very little about the geography of Des Moines except the area surrounding our home and the central business district. When someone in the family purchased a weekly pass for the streetcars, I could use it on Sunday to go "streetcar riding" to the outskirts of the city.

Dad 's job as janitor in a men's clothing store gave him access to discarded material. Many customers left their old shoes in the store after purchasing new ones, and he rescued them from the trash and brought home those that were still usable. After being sterilized by steam, they were quite stiff and brittle but wearable. When holes appeared in the bottom, rubber soles from the dime store were cemented to the worn ones. We rarely bought toilet tissue — the tissue used to pack new hats served very well after it was "straightened out" (one of my tasks). Bare feet were the norm in the summer, and new clothing was usually a special gift reserved for Easter. Haircuts were provided by my brother Inman, even after he moved into a boardinghouse. Thanks to my mother's skill with a sewing machine, worn clothing was repaired, cut down, or recycled in the family until it was threadbare. We had three kinds of clothing: "good" clothes that were worn primarily on Sunday, school clothes that were changed immediately upon returning from school, and after-school clothes. The latter were sometimes tattered and patched, but overalls or patched clothes were never worn to school. In my later years, I viewed with some amusement the "me-too generation" practice of buying and wearing "preworn" clothing with conspicuous holes as a cross-generational attempt to gain attention and express their independence.

We bought and processed live chickens, and learned to manage with the cheaper cuts of meat — beef heart, meat loaf (equal parts of ground beef, pork, and veal with plenty of bread crumbs, delicious spices and herbs, and eggs to hold it together), pig ears and tails, ham hocks instead of ham, bacon ends and pieces instead of center slices, and pork instead of beef liver — no chit'lins, though; Mother wouldn't have them in the house! Mother made delicious bread, but we also bought "day-old" (unsold and returned from the retail store after who knows how many days) sandwich bread from Ungles bakery on Center Street. Larger quantities of fruit and vegetables for canning were purchased at the City Market at 2nd and Locust, and the streetcar motormen and bus drivers were used to seeing me waiting at the corner with a bushel of peaches or other fruit. I placed the basket near the long seats over the front wheel, and someone met me when the car stopped up the street from our house. Shelves in the basement were lined with jars of fruit, jelly, preserves, and piccalilli that Mother canned, and large crocks full of homemade sourkraut sat in a corner. The piccalilli was appreciated when Jack Frost arrived and beans became a staple in our diet: navy, great northern, lima, pinto, red, black, and kidney beans, baked with molasses, and black-eyed peas. We boys sometimes recited a little ditty: "Beans, beans, the musical fruit; the more you eat the more you poot. The more you poot the better you feel, so let's have beans for every meal."

In the spring and summer, we gratefully switched to boiled wild greens (mustard, dandelions, lamb's-quarter, dock, young plantain) with corn bread and enjoyed garden produce in season. And fresh tomatoes — ahh!

Looking back from the relative prosperity of the late twentieth century with more safety nets for the least fortunate families, one might conclude that such spartan rigor was humiliating and thus resented, but that was not at all true. Our method of coping may have been unique to our family, but we knew that others throughout the nation were obliged to find their own ways to cope. We were proud to own our modest home, maintain its cream-colored paint with chocolate-brown trim in excellent condition, and always have plenty to eat, even if it was inexpensive fare.

We disdained public welfare (called "relief" in those days) as essentially a Faustian pact with the devil that fostered dependence, a negative self-image, and invaded privacy. Our good health also helped, of course. We were certainly not deprived; rather we were affluent in terms of love and support from family and friends. Once when I came home from school, where reference had been made to poor people, I asked Mother, "Are we poor?" Her answer was quick and direct. "Yes, and it's inconvenient, but it is not a disgrace."

Although their presence cannot be blamed on the depression, mosquitoes were common in the oppressive summer heat that drove us outdoors. Lacking air-conditioning or screens on our windows, we repulsed mosquitoes by burning rags; the smoke would keep them at bay while we slept on the open porch. When we finally had the money, a side porch was screened in to provide a refuge from both bites and smoke.

The sacrifice of Mother's teaching career for the sake of her children was rewarded as we completed high school, and especially when Inman earned two degrees from the University of Iowa, working his way through the university in the same way that many African American men did at the time. He shined shoes at Short's shoe repair shop on Clinton Street facing Sheaffer Hall, and did janitorial work at Ford Hopkins's drugstore to earn his meals at their lunch counter. Haywood Short had moved to Iowa City from Missouri several years earlier and established a shoe repair business, hiring African American shoemakers from Missouri and university students as shoe shiners. He was an astute businessman and invested in real estate in downtown Iowa City as well as on the edge of the city. His grandson, Haywood Belle, now manages the properties.

All of my family gave me their full encouragement and moral support as I prepared for higher education. Financial support was out of the question; in fact, I paid for my room and board at home when I started working regularly after school at age sixteen, not because of greed on the part of my parents but rather because the family was barely eking out a living with every member working seven days a week. I graduated from North High in January 1939, and expanded my after-school job in the Savery Hotel to full-time plus — twelve hours a day, seven days a week. My boss was Lloyd Shelton, an acquaintance of my brother Inman, who managed a shoe-shine stand in the basement men's room next to a barber shop that was later moved upstairs. In lieu of paying rent for the shoe-shine "franchise," we cleaned the washroom, the toilets, the barber shop (later the billiard parlor), and the main hallway. I became an expert at swinging a thirty-two-ounce mop and exterminating cockroaches the size of mice. There was very little money or time for the pursuit of mischief, but my education was advanced considerably by tending the footwear of the affluent, meeting the prizefight crowd that haunted the billiard hall, and developing skill at billiards after hours. As a bonus, I was able to see some prizefights by carrying gym bags for the fighters. I particularly remember Johnny Paycheck, who later gained fame by succumbing to the lethal punches of Joe Louis in thirty-two seconds. My sex education until then had consisted of reading

Vivilore in our home library, and Lloyd Shelton completed it by informing me that "a woman's nature is in her stomach." I didn't know exactly what that meant, but I knew that he was not referring to the digestive tract.

People have asked me whether I resented doing dreary and low-paid work during that period. My answer is no — I considered the temporary inconvenience as an investment in a desirable future. Those teen years had their pleasures, of course. I went with Mother to see *Gone With the Wind* when it first came out, a fond memory because it was the only time I went to a movie with either parent. It ranks with a later experience when I accompanied my daughter Chris to visit American University in Washington, D.C., and we went to see *Dr. Zhivago* at a theater east of the White House. My guest for the high school graduation banquet in Younkers Tea Room was Naomi Walden, a very pretty girl from Highland Park in northwest Des Moines. I attended the banquet with a red eye: I must have been nervous in preparing for my first date, because I put a big glob of soap in it.

My friends included Laurene Jones, niece of Laurence C. Jones, a graduate of the University of Iowa in 1907 and founder of Piney Woods Country School in Mississippi. I admired him as a model of selfless service to his fellow humans, and President Virgil M. Hancher eventually named him as one of the university's ten most distinguished alumni. In late 1939, she introduced me to her best friend and my future wife, Wynonna Griffin of West Des Moines, and we soon began to date exclusively. Since I had no car, visiting her home meant a forty-five-minute ride on streetcars, later replaced by buses. That was a problem because I had to observe Dad's strict eleven o'clock evening curfew. Normally, I would have taken the West Des Moines bus to a transfer point downtown, then proceeded home on the Clark Street bus. To save time when I was late, I left the first bus at the point nearest our house, and then sprinted for more than a mile to get home on time. Our principal entertainment was attending movies and listening to music, often with a group of friends. I still marvel at how we managed to be happy with so little money to spend, but teenagers in love could live happily in a desert. Wynonna's neighbor, who

I once viewed as a rival for her affections, had the interesting name Clifford Lovelady. With a Lovelady to choose from, I don't know why she settled for a mere Hubbard.

I became well acquainted with Wynonna's parents, Robert and Edna Griffin, her brother Robert, and her foster sister Maxine Anderson, who later worked with the Red Cross in India. Robert went to Virginia Union College and spent most of his career working for the Internal Revenue Service and in the Postal Service. Mr. Griffin worked as a bag filler for the nearby portland cement factory, and Mrs. Griffin managed the household and carefully allocated the weekly paycheck that her husband simply turned over to her. Their home was modest, with an outdoor toilet and space heaters in the living and dining rooms that had to heat the entire house. He had an unusual habit of never referring to his wife by name, using third-person pronouns that had to be interpreted in the context of the situation.

The Griffins were devout members of the tiny Mt. Hebron Baptist Church less than a block from their home, and I enjoyed attending some of the services and seeing how much their religion meant to Wynonna's parents. They were happy to comply with Reverend Garrett's insistence as a dinner guest on having his dessert served before the rest of the dinner; he wanted "to leave the table with the taste of meat in my mouth." Mr. Griffin was one of the deacons who passed the collection plate and counted the amount. The senior deacon would then announce to the congregation of a few dozen: "We have $18.37: let's pass the plate again and bring it up to $20." If one more pass did not meet the goal, the plate was passed a third time. I had already contributed to my own Methodist Church, but found a little more to help with the charming procedure.

In retrospect, my experience in Des Moines was a fortuitous preparation for a career in a rapidly evolving and diverse world, and my life's work has been decisively influenced by having operated comfortably in two distinct but overlapping societies. My family provided personal and spiritual nurturing, and relied on the schools only to develop my academic and social skills. The unpitying school of experience taught me other skills necessary to succeed, not merely survive, in the real world. Wherever I go, I do not feel like a stranger because of my cultural background — in my travels to every continent except Australia and

Antarctica and in my contacts with people from many nations, I have seen that all human beings are a single family. Virtues and evils, however defined, are distributed widely in this great family, and one cannot identify who is "good" and who is "bad" by examining their ancestry or geographic origins. I also appreciate the profound influence of individual experience on one's development; I often think, seeing exceptional acts of virtue or evil, "There but for the Grace of God go I." When I see any person, I can say, "I can do something better than that person, and on the other hand that person can do something better than I can." A realistic attitude and a sense of humor also help, because I have not found life to be a rose garden.

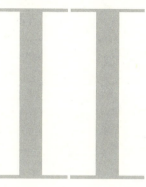

The Engineering Years

Off to College

When I graduated from high school, nearby Drake University offered me a half-tuition scholarship that I could not accept because the other half was far beyond my means. Choosing my life work presented a serious problem; I do not even know whether there was a counselor in North High. Much later, when I tried to recruit minority students for college, I learned that the advice of school counselors is often counterproductive for talented minority students — the advice, if any, presumes a continuation of the status quo with severely limited opportunities, regardless of academic performance.

Careers for African Americans were restricted by the practices of racial discrimination just as careers for women were limited by gender bias, so planning was a solitary and dismal task. Careers controlled by the Establishment, such as corporate management, government, the military, education, banking, and finance were therefore eliminated from consideration. I considered medicine and law because success in those fields depends more on patients and clients than on the power structure, but reluctantly eliminated them because they required education beyond four years and I had no financial base from which to operate. I note in passing that doctors and lawyers in Iowa did not have to rely exclusively on the black community for clients and patients. Their clients included many white people who chose black professionals for reasons of their own. The clergy was eliminated for the same reason my father departed from a family tradition: I was not "called." Although I could not have articulated it at that time, I was also uncomfortable with the church's passive acceptance of a grossly unfair status quo with the hope that a better world was in store after death. My decision might have been different if Martin Luther King Jr.'s vision of religion as an instrument of social action had been expressed a generation earlier.

I settled on engineering because it represented an intellectual challenge, could be completed in four years, was well suited to my temperament, and offered the possibility of a career somewhat less affected by racial bias. That hope was probably inspired by having met Archie Alexander, a black Des Moines engineer who had been an All-American football player at the University of Iowa; I was one of a small group of teenagers he invited to his home when I was in high school. He was a partner in an engineering firm that designed the utility tunnel system for the University of Iowa and some of the major bridges across the Potomac River in Washington, D.C. President Eisenhower later appointed him governor of the Virgin Islands.

With a savings account of $252.50 amassed from shoe-shining income at a few dollars per week (I still have the bank savings book showing deposits and withdrawals when tuition was due), I enrolled in the College of Engineering at the University of Iowa in 1940. I continued my craft at a vacant stand in the basement men's room of the Hotel Jefferson in Iowa City; the shoe-shine stand offered an unplanned benefit by providing a quiet place to study during the many hours when no customers were available. When the hotel manager saw that I was a reliable operator, he built a new stand with a cabinet where I could store my books while away on other business. A v-12 program for training navy airmen was at the university then, and the young officers occasionally stopped to get a shoe shine. While I was shining his shoes, one of them looked at the book I had been reading — *Principles of Chemical Engineering*. He inquired, "Are you studying this?" In response to my affirmative reply, he gave me a $5 bill — enough to feed me for a week. The income from shining shoes provided $20 a month for a room and one meal a day at the home of Carl and Frances Culberson at 713 South Capitol Street, next to the railroad tracks. If the income was sufficient, I ate other meals at various restaurants, including Vivian's Chicken Shack on Burlington Street.

I knew the Culbersons before coming to college because Frances's brother, Adam Johnson Sr., was a neighbor in Des Moines and his children had been among my close friends. Their grandparents, Adam and Martha Johnson, had migrated from slavery in the cotton fields of Tennessee to Knox County, Illinois, and then in the 1880s bought a farm of 160 acres near the town of Gravity in Taylor County, Iowa. Frances, Adam, and their sisters Lulu and Virginia were born on that farm, and Lulu Johnson became the first African American woman to earn a Ph.D. from an American university. The achievement won her recognition from the University of Iowa Alumni Association at a special luncheon in her honor in 1991. I knew of Lulu's scholarship long before I went to college, and have admired her ever since.

Although I chose a living arrangement in a private home for financial reasons, it was the norm for African American men because we were not permitted to live in housing provided by the university, even though some black students were recruited varsity athletes, recognized as All-Big-Ten and All-American. Two of my roommates were All-Big-Ten athletes — Lee Farmer of Maywood, Illinois, was a champion sprinter and broad jumper, and Jim Walker of Gary, Indiana, played tackle on the Hawkeye "Ironman" team. Although African Americans were on the early teams, they were not taken on road trips if the host team objected to playing against them. Even that level of acceptance was absent in basketball, however, as incredible as it seems in the light of today's sports scene. The first African American to play on the varsity basketball team was Iowa City native Richard (Bud) Culberson, who transferred from Virginia Union College in 1944 to play on the first Hawkeye team to win a clear Big Ten title. Athletes apparently were accepted by their teammates in all team activities, but the races went their separate ways for most social events.

Most of the women lived in a house at 942 Iowa Avenue that was owned and operated by the Iowa Federation of Colored Women's Clubs and which met the university requirement for "approved housing." Exclusion from university-sponsored events was offensive, but we compensated by organizing our own social activities, with considerable success. On special occasions such as homecoming, we had formal dinner-dances with live music at the D and L Restaurant downtown or at the Mayflower Inn on North Dubuque Street, subsidized by alumni. We especially liked the small band led by Larry Barrett, who was a regular performer on radio station WSUI and who later married Ann Gerber, the daughter of my good friend and colleague, Professor John Gerber.

After joining Kappa Alpha Psi fraternity during my sophomore year, I lived in the home of Chester and Estelle Ferguson, which served as a chapter house. "Mother Ferg" was loved by all, and she was the first person elected to the Black Hall of Fame, located in a lounge of the Iowa Memorial Union. I pleased her and my three roommates by furnishing our room with curtains that Mother made from an old bedspread. Fraternity life was quite conventional, including hazing pledges by requiring them to retrieve an object at midnight from the statue of a black angel in the cemetery.

Why did African Americans endure unfair treatment without protest or petitioning for reform? There is no single answer, but we had no reason to believe that complaints would lead to anything other than a suggestion that we go elsewhere if the conditions were unacceptable. After all, the university viewed us as visitors rather than full members of the general community. We knew of no avenue for legal redress, and the later experience of civil rights protesters confirmed that laws were not on the protesters' side. Moreover, we took the view that our misery was transitory — we could endure it for a few years because an education was seen as the way to a better future. College was not merely a pleasant interlude between a sheltered childhood and an assured career; for many of us it was the only feasible route out of poverty and oppression.

My move to Iowa City presented an uncomfortable problem. The AME Church of my ancestors was moribund in Iowa City and lacked a regular congregation, although it owned a frame house that was later placed on the national roster of historic buildings. Occasionally a visiting minister from Cedar Rapids conducted services at Bethel in Iowa City, but that was an inadequate substitute for my regular participation at St. Paul AME Church in Des Moines. Not seeing a strong distinction between denominations, I occasionally attended the Baptist Church at the corner of Clinton and Burlington Streets, and soon joined the First United Methodist Church and participated regularly in the programs of the Wesley Foundation ministry to college students. I knew that the AME Church had been established in 1816 by African Americans led by Richard Allen, who had expected to be part of the Methodist Episcopal Church. When they were effectively rejected by the white congregation in Philadelphia in 1787, a group created a separate denomination. If Bethel had been active, I would have joined AME, but time marches on, and I was comfortable in First Methodist, which has been my home church ever since.

The College of Engineering was a fortunate choice because its faculty and students treated my enrollment as a normal event, in contrast with the chilly reception reported by students enrolled in some of the other majors. Dean Francis M. Dawson was remarkably supportive; soon after my arrival, he called me to his office without explanation, welcomed me, and quizzed me about my financial resources for educational costs. I informed him of the arrangements I had made, and we discussed my educational plans. Quietly and inconspicuously, the gentle dean from Nova Scotia became another "guardian angel," recommending me for a supplementary work/study job at the Iowa Institute of Hydraulic Research (IIHR), and occasionally inviting me to his home. Eventually he assisted my discharge from the army in 1945 by arranging for me to work on classified war research in the Engineering and Physics Departments, and financed the purchase of our first home in 1947 when the banks declined to do so.

Dawson was also director of the IIHR, with a research specialty of improving the efficiency and safety of plumbing systems. Flush toilets that were sawed in half with windows to view the internal flow occupied a prominent position on the main-floor hydraulics laboratory, and the predictable comment of viewers was "They must be for half-assed people." His research findings led to substantial changes in building codes; when I see the vents on the roofs of every home and commercial building, I think of his award-winning research to prevent sewer gases from entering interior buildings and to prevent back siphoning of contaminated water into the supply line.

When I began working at the institute as a freshman, it was well on its way to achieving a worldwide reputation for excellence in teaching as well as research under the direction of the associate director, Professor Hunter Rouse, who succeeded Dawson as director in 1944 and in 1972 became one of the first five faculty named to Carver Professorships. He never seemed to notice my ethnic background except for an amused suggestion that I might simply say "no" and "yes" rather than "yes, sir" or "yes, ma'am," which was customary for children in our family when addressing people in an older generation. The head of the related Department of Mechanics and Hydraulics was Professor Joseph W. Howe, whose long and extraordinarily complete record of rainfall and runoff in the Ralston Creek watershed serves as a database for many other researchers. My duties involved running a ditto machine in his office as well as taking data and helping the mechanical staff at the institute. Both Rouse and Howe joined Dawson as my lifelong friends, and they were responsible for providing opportunities and guidance to promote my career development.

In view of the roles played by Dawson, Rouse, Howe, Professor Willard "Sandy" Boyd, and others in my life, I refer to a statement made by Isaac Newton, the father of classical mechanics and an inventor of calculus. In a letter to Robert Hooke dated February 5, 1675/76, he wrote, "If I have seen further [than Hooke and René Descartes] it is by standing on the shoulders of giants." The "giant's shoulder" metaphor was not original to Newton, however: Seneca, in the first century, had observed that a pygmy does not become a giant by standing on the shoulder of one.

In some respects the environment of my undergraduate years was a continuation of the Des Moines experience. Off campus, I joined and became president of Kappa Alpha Psi, a black fraternity in a segregated Greek system, I was a regular participant in the weekly "Negro Forum," and I established lasting friendships with many African Americans from various regions and academic disciplines. Later, when I returned from the army, Eloise Usher (later Belcher), a graduate student in theater, needed an African American for a key role in her play *Jacob's Ladder* and invited me to play opposite her. I accepted and enjoyed the unfamiliar experience as a thespian. Eloise went on to join the faculty at Spelman College in Atlanta and later taught at South Carolina State College in Orangeburg.

When I enrolled in 1940, the environment for students had changed very little from Herbert Jenkins's description in his 1933 master's thesis. He reported that in addition to exclusion from university-owned residences and restrictions on athletic teams, African American students were often assigned certain seats in classrooms according to the whim of the instructor, and excluded from university-sponsored social events if any student objected to their presence. A simple request excused us from the "mandatory" ROTC requirement, apparently because the army was not interested in recruiting minority officers. We were denied access to most university employment because, as explained by the library director, "There might have been the possibility of colored applicants being classed with foreign students; furthermore, it is generally the policy to give work to those in the majority." There were no overall university or city guidelines for the rights of minority students, so we were at the mercy of the least tolerant person in the area of concern: if anyone objected, then the student's request was denied. This applied not only to university resources, but also to off-campus employment, housing, and service at private businesses such as restaurants and retail shops.

Despite discriminatory practices in some parts of the community, my classmates, all white, were congenial, included me in all academic activities, and we worked effectively in the teams traditionally used in engineering education. When fellow students warned me against a major in chemical engineering because of its difficulty, I promptly selected it in spite of having had no previous work in chemistry; it was not even taught at North High. I reasoned that the toughest major should offer the greatest reward for successful completion, and I was not looking for an easy course of study. The results of the first chemistry test were sobering; my score of 22 percent was the nadir of all my school years, but I persisted and received the junior prize in chemistry. I was selected for membership and served as an officer in honorary societies for students in engineering (Tau Beta Pi), chemistry (Phi Lambda Upsilon), and electrical engineering (Eta Kappa Nu), and learned more inspirational initiation songs in the process. The Tau Beta Pi initiation included an interesting example of intellectual hazing: initiates spent an entire day taking a difficult written test that covered a wide range of subjects from art to religion to zoology. The thick notebook of our answers was duly collected by the members and presumably sent away for grading. When we later inquired about how well we had done, the answer was "No one ever looks at the answers; it was just an exercise."

The instructors were unbiased in their teaching and grading, and Professor Thomas Farrell, who taught Engineering English, appreciated my knowledge of mythology from my eclectic childhood reading habits. He complimented my work but awarded me a "B" because of his conviction that freshmen could not do "A" work; in contrast, a colleague who taught the other section of the same course gave "A's" to most of his students. I didn't complain because I had heard this in advance, and did not place a great importance on grades. Farrell was a strict taskmaster, and insisted that students write in clear and well-organized English. Some students did not appreciate the rigor, and converted a long pole into a slender seven-foot-long cone with barbed hooks along the sides. They painted it a garish purple and arranged a formal ceremony at which they presented Farrell with "The Royal Order of the Purple Shaft." Farrell had the last laugh, however. Several graduates wrote back after a few years on the job to thank him for developing skills that earned them promotions over colleagues who were competent technologists but did not present the results of their work in intelligible English.

Although we were reasonably satisfied with the quality of our instruction, the engineering students wanted to inform teachers of which ones students considered better and which teachers were less effective. Students in the honorary engineering student society, Tau Beta Pi, of which I was recording secretary with Bill Bauer as president, consulted with some faculty members and devised a survey form to evaluate teaching effectiveness. Near the end of each semester, the instructor would

*Rosa Belle Wallace,
high school graduation,
1907.*

*Community band, Macon, Philip Alexander Hubbard kneeling at far
left, ca. 1920.*

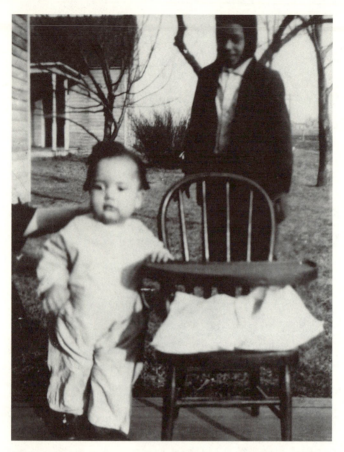

Philip G. Hubbard, age one, with brother E. W., age thirteen, 1922.

Washington Irving ninth grade class of 1936. I am in the front row, sixth from the right.

First date Naomi Walden, left, with my future wife,
Wynonna Griffin, 1939.

With roommates Lee Farmer and Jim Walker, 1943.

Just married and in the army, 1943.

EE-7 GRADUATING CLASS
June 8, 1944

LAWTHER BROWN BENTLEY SULZER MILLER BROSIG STOKLEY BRAUNECK SLACK WAHL KALLEHOORF PETERSON HOGAN
RAU THOMPSON RESNICK HUBBARD HIRICH MENDENHALL SANDELIN WELSER WAND HIATT HYLAND

Army ASTP class at graduation, 1944.

Revived Kappa Alpha Psi Fraternity, 1947.

Explaining the hot-wire anemometer, 1951.

Opposite. Demonstrating the hot-wire anemometer with a jet-suspended ball as prop, ca. 1955.

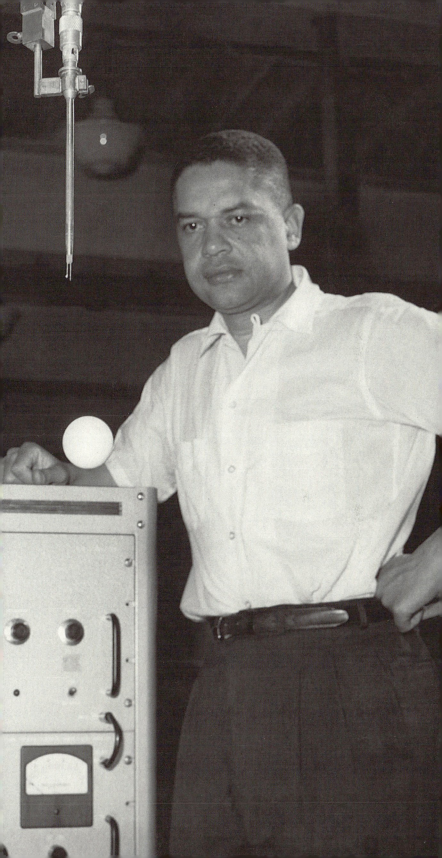

*A growing family:
Peter and Richard in front,
Christine, Michael, and Philip
in back, 1956.*

Monica, Philip Jr., Anthony, and Susan Hubbard.

Opposite. Wynonna, 1980.

Matthew, Chris, and Jim Walters.

Michael Hubbard, Sarah Hubbard, Carol Torres, and Peter Torres.

Richard Hubbard and Alaka Wali with Eric and Shanti Hubbard.

Peter and Mary Hubbard with Robert (top), Katherine, and Neil.

The family home at 4 West Park Road.

Opposite. At work in Old Capitol, 1966.

Iowa Coordinating Council for Post-secondary Education, 1980.

Board of Fellows, University of Iowa School of Religion, 1988.

Academy of Distinguished Engineering Alumni, original class, 1997.
Front row, left to right: Lilia Abrons, James Ashton, Thomas Daniels,
Himie Voxman, and Lucille Smith representing her late husband, Rob-
ert. Back row, left to right: Philip Hubbard, Gregs Thomopulos repre-
senting the late C. Maxwell Stanley, Gary Seamans, Darrell Wyrick,
Frank Chrencik, Margaret Petersen, and Mikio Arie.

Opposite. Portrait by Cloy Kent, 1981.

Reading to grandchildren Neil, Katherine, and Robert, 1989.
Photo by Tom Jorgensen.

Katherine and Grandpa at the park, 1991.

leave the class and a student member of the society would dis-
tribute and then collect the completed surveys. Officers of Tau
Beta Pi compiled a statistical summary of the anonymous surveys and gave each instructor a copy of his (all were men then)
summary for such use as he chose. Instructors wanted to benefit from good evaluations and included them in their performance reports. Much later, when I was chair of the University
Council on Teaching, the process was developed by the evaluation service to a highly sophisticated state; they now administer
evaluations for 2,600 courses in all departments.

For reasons that predated my arrival, engineering and law
students carried on a continuing feud, each side using its specialized skills. On one occasion, engineers brought a horse and
wagon to the law building in the wee hours of the morning,
dismantled the wagon, and reassembled it on the roof. Reason-
ing that a wagon was useless without a horse, they walked the
horse up the stairs to the roof, knowing full well that horses will
go up, but not down, stairs. Someone reversed the original procedure to return the wagon to the street, but only a crane with
a sling could restore Dobbin to terra firma. The lawyers retali-
ated during the engineers' MECCA week celebration by kidnap-
ping the MECCA queen and wining and dining her royally while
the engineers at the MECCA ball fumed in frustration. (Honest,
that's the way the story was told to me.)

World War II was raging in Europe as I studied, and owing
to the knowledge and insight of Rouse, the Iowa Institute of
Hydraulic Research launched several projects of basic research
that contributed to the solution of critical wartime problems.
The army and navy sponsored research on the drag of station-
ary ships in flowing water; the pressure distribution around
cylindrical objects such as underwater torpedoes; air-tunnel
studies of fog dispersal for military airfields (critically important in the Battle of London); the diffusion of smoke and gas
in urban areas; the wind structure over mountainous terrain;
water-tunnel investigations of cavitation around underwater
bodies; and development of firefighting monitors (equipment
to support nozzles) for naval vessels.

America entered the war after the attack on Pearl Harbor
during my sophomore year. On Dad's advice in summer 1942, I
joined the army's Enlisted Reserve Corps, which was supposed

to defer me from active service until I could complete my college education. The deferment was only temporary, and I was ordered to report for active duty on May 11, 1943.

Before reporting to Camp Dodge, however, I married my fellow student and fiancée of two years, Wynonna Marie Griffin of West Des Moines. We had been dating each other exclusively since being introduced by her friend Laurene Jones four years earlier. We had simply expected to marry at some unspecified time, but the call to active duty set the date. We were also aware that my army salary would include a small stipend for a wife, which would help Wynonna with expenses. I would have preferred for Wynonna to stay in college, but she chose to live with her parents and worked in a factory making army gloves; marriage was the only career she wanted.

In retrospect, I note that our decision to marry was made in sharp contrast to the conventional process. Financial resources never entered the picture, because we had never had excess money and did not see that financial security was necessary. Both families agreed with our decision, and we had faith that two people completely dedicated to each other could overcome any obstacles together. That is one example of a general feature of my life: my hopes and dreams, as well as my security, relate to people rather than to material things. The very simple wedding on May 3 (Rev. Elmer Diercks, best man Joe Howard, and the two of us) was performed at Roger Williams Fellowship, the Baptist student center near campus. The building where we were married was subsequently purchased by the university to house its admissions outreach activities and renamed Bowman House. Wynonna's parents gave her a sky-blue dress, my favorite color, for the wedding. In order to buy a decent suit and a wedding ring for Wynonna I pawned the massive gold watch inherited from my father, who had inherited it from his uncle. The inscription in the watch said "To Rev. Philip A. Hubbard from the AME Church, St. Joseph, Missouri, April 15, 1884." The pawnbroker recognized the importance of my heirloom, and kept it safe until I could reclaim it after my army service. Later, I passed it on to my oldest son.

4

Slide Rules Can't Shoot

At Camp Dodge near Des Moines, I was examined physically and mentally and sent to basic training at the Engineer Replacement Training Center, Company B, 35th E.T. battalion, Fort Leonard Wood, Missouri. I was once again in an all-black environment with men principally from South Carolina and Georgia. Our sergeant was a career soldier, and impressed me by his air of professional competence. I was also impressed by the regular meals, and gained sixteen pounds of solid weight in thirteen weeks of strenuous physical activity and constant griping about the "awful army food"; on the many occasions when mutton was served, we insisted that it was goat meat. Many years later, when I spent a summer in Argentina, I learned that a young goat, barbecued on a vertical spit prominently displayed in a restaurant window, was a real delicacy. I also discovered an unsuspected talent — the ability to sleep under adverse conditions. On a long hike in the hills, I could lie down on the rocks, put my helmet liner under my head, go to sleep immediately, and wake up refreshed at the end of a ten-minute break.

Although basic training was normally completed in nine weeks, I continued for a total of thirteen weeks because I had been assigned to the Army Specialized Training Program that prepared soldiers for critically needed specialties. At the Specialized Training and Reassignment unit at Grinnell College, I studied college-level refresher courses for a short time and was soon sent to Penn State for advanced study in electrical engineering rather than my Iowa major of chemical engineering. Once again, I was the fly in the buttermilk — the only minority student in the class. State College was a pleasant community, and my class of fifteen men lived in a fraternity house that was vacant because the usual occupants had gone off to war. We marched to classes, and I played the baritone horn in the marching band after four years without practice. Thankfully, my sour notes were drowned out by the tubas.

After a short time, Wynonna came to State College and lived in the nearby home of the university treasurer, William Hostetter, in exchange for assisting with the housework. The Hostetters were Pennsylvania Dutch, and we felt comfortable around them with our Midwest background. In our spare time, Wynonna and I took long walks in the beautiful Alleghenies, and visited New York City when I had a furlough. It was our first visit to a metropolis, and we stayed at the Hotel Theresa in Harlem, visited the Statue of Liberty, and saw some of the usual tourist attractions.

I completed the army program in electrical engineering with honors on schedule in May 1944 and was selected by our officers to receive the class award for outstanding leadership. The graduates were promoted to private first class and assigned to regular army duties, some with the signal corps and others with the Manhattan Engineering District. The latter were the envy of the unit because we assumed that they would live in New York City, but everyone was surprised when the name turned out to be the code designation for the atomic energy facility in the hills of Tennessee. I was assigned to the 372nd infantry regiment in Camp Breckinridge, Kentucky, an all-black unit that had been activated from National Guard battalions in Massachusetts, Ohio, and New Jersey, Headquarters Company from Washington, D.C., and Service Company from Baltimore. The commanding officer was Col. Edward O. "Ned" Gourdin, a former Olympic broad jumper, who later became the first black Superior Court judge in the state of Massachusetts.

Soon after my arrival, Gourdin sent for me, with my army

record on his desk. He apparently thought I was something of an oddity.

"So you are from Iowa. Do you know Charles Brookins?" (Brookins was an alumnus of the university, and Iowa's first black Olympian in track.)

"No, sir, but I have heard of him."

"How about Duke Slater?" (Slater was an Iowa All-American football lineman, and was later a judge in Chicago.)

"Yes, sir, he is a native of Clinton, and my relatives there are his good friends."

"Please give him my regards the next time you see him. . . . I see that you scored 152 on the Army General Classification (IQ) test, completed the four-year ASTP engineering course with honors, and Major Tidmore rated you at the head of the class when considered as officer candidate material. Why were you sent to the infantry?" (The question was purely academic, because as a black career officer he knew the army's logic better than I did.)

"Sir, I only received orders to report, no explanation."

"Well, you are assigned to Capt. O. J. Wines's Headquarters Company where we can keep an eye on you. Sergeant Burleigh will show you what your duties are, but you will have more use for a rifle than a slide rule."

And that was very true. Once again, I was crawling under barbed wire and over obstacle courses.

On June 22, 1944, I received word that my brother Inman had been killed by a double bolt of lightning on a hill in Italy, where his signal corps company was stationed after the invasion of Italy. In a period of a few weeks, the number of Rosa Belle's sons to graduate from college had increased from one to two, then, in a flash, back to one. He was a sergeant major — with a master's degree in chemistry from the University of Iowa and experience in teaching, he might have been a commissioned officer, except for his color. His body is now buried in the Sicily-Rome military cemetery at Nettuno, on the Mediterranean Sea sixty kilometers south of Rome, but he lives on in the hearts of his family. My niece Paula Taylor of Davenport (Paul's daughter) located Inman's grave and visited it around 1994. Inman's widow, Olivia Merriwether Perkins, still lives in St. Louis, which had been their home since they were married. Inman's death led our family to place its hopes for an educated member on me, and I could not disappoint them.

In the fall the 372nd (in army lingo, the "trey-natural-deuce") was moved to Fort Huachuca, Arizona, presumably in preparation for action in the Pacific theater. The long train loaded with men and matériel painted or dyed olive green crawled over the impressively wide Mississippi River, through Texarkana, and endless miles of Texas sagebrush, jackrabbits, armadillos, and an occasional person. Fort Huachuca was near the Mexican border, and the soldiers occasionally visited the tiny town of Agua Prieta from which they brought "agua" that would set a goat on fire; tequila must be distilled from jalapeño peppers. On a rare occasion I met a Women's Army Corps (WAC) officer named Consuela Bland from Keokuk, apparently the only other Iowan for hundreds of miles. Usually, the only women or parts of women we saw were at a great distance or in crude homemade eight-millimeter films — no rag or bone, just a hank o' hair.

I can recall only a few of the names of my fellow soldiers from more than a half century ago. Private Willis Byrd and I survived basic training together, and he later earned a Ph.D. at Iowa. M.Sgt. Harry T. Burleigh III from Washington, D.C., brings an illustrious musical family to mind. His grandfather, Harry Thacker Burleigh I (1866–1949), was a professional soloist and composed or arranged more than 200 songs and spirituals, including "Deep River," "Swing Low, Sweet Chariot," and "Go Tell It on the Mountain." While he was a student at the National Conservatory of Music, Burleigh introduced Antonin Dvořák to Negro spirituals when the latter was a guest of the State Department, preparing to compose the New World Symphony. M.Sgt. Felix Goodwin was promoted to commissioned officer in the field after I left, eventually retired as lieutenant colonel, then served for many years as assistant to the president of the University of Arizona. Some of the more unusual names impressed me because military ranks and initials without names were rather common: privates General Lee Thompson and Major George Wilson, for example. The army's insistence on uniformity led to some interesting results: if someone had no middle name, he was entered, for example, as William (NMI) Jackson, with NMI standing for "no middle initial." One soldier whose complete name was R B Jones was originally recorded as R(only) B(only) Jones so that the army's need for uniformity could be satisfied. A later typist apparently saw no need for the parentheses, and the soldier was thereafter in the official record as Ronly Bonly Jones.

We usually had sand in our shoes, but the call to action never came and it was rumored that it never would — soldiers were being discharged in large numbers following the end of the war in Europe. Impatient with simply marking time, I took the examination for Officer Candidate School. Soon the executive officer, Lt. Col. Herbert Barrow, summoned me:

"Your score on the exam was a perfect 150, so you obviously qualify for OCS, but upon completion you will merely be assigned to an officer pool because the army has begun to demobilize."

I didn't like the idea of cooling my heels in an officer pool. "Sir, is there any way I could be discharged so I could make a contribution as a civilian?"

"I don't know of anything, and I'm sure that the army will release you only if there is a guarantee that you will be doing important work related to the war. If you find a possibility, let me know." I wrote immediately to Dean Dawson, and he quickly responded that my skills were needed in classified research at the university, but time was of the essence. With the letter in hand, Colonel Barrow arranged to expedite my discharge, and on January 23, 1945, I headed for Jefferson Barracks (the discharge center in St. Louis) and Iowa. It appeared that the colonels in the 372nd had joined many others as my guardian angels. After I left, the regiment was sent to Hawaii.

Family Life

Upon arriving in Iowa City, I hurried to Dean Dawson's office to ask whether I had made the deadline because his message had emphasized the urgency of the need. He responded that the need was indeed urgent, but he was familiar with the deliberate pace of army procedures and had wanted to discourage red tape delays by implying a deadline. (He had fought as an ANZAC [soldiers from Australia, New Zealand, and Canada] in World War I, where he met and married his gracious and dignified English wife Letitia. I was amused by their custom when driving: she rode in the backseat of their green Packard while he drove.)

The classified research project that brought me back to Iowa City involved the development of two devices that could help the troops who were still fighting and dying in the Pacific theater, and we worked diligently in the hope that we could solve the problems quickly. The devices were a toss-bomb mechanism that enabled a fighter plane to launch bombs accurately using its regular gunsight, and a proximity fuse that detonated mortar shells shortly before they landed. The project was terminated after the end of the war in the Pacific, and one of the research staff, George Carsner, remained in the Physics Department and helped build instruments for James Van Allen's pioneering space exploration.

To qualify for a bachelor's degree, I took correspondence courses in accounting and economics that had not been required for the army certificate, and received my B.S. degree in electrical engineering in January 1946. Although the research project had been terminated, I remained at the university to pursue an advanced degree in chemical engineering, which had been my major for the first three years of undergraduate study. Benefits from the GI bill covered my educational expenses, and I worked as a research engineer at the Iowa Institute of Hydraulic Research to earn living expenses. Studying in one field and working in another proved to be an inefficient use of time, so I switched my major to mechanics and hydraulics, since I had no particular plans to use either degree.

The postwar years were perhaps the happiest, busiest, and most productive period of our lives. Our first home was in an apartment on the second floor of a house at 9 East Prentiss, owned by Roy and Wilda Hester, who lived on the first floor. Roy repaired shoes in Short's Shoe Repair, and then worked as a janitor in the Iowa Memorial Union after the repair shop was closed. Wilda was an Iowa alumna and an adviser to the local chapter of Alpha Kappa Alpha sorority. Similarly, their next-door neighbor Allan Lemme repaired shoes at Short's, and his wife Helen advised Delta Sigma Theta sorority, rival to AKA. Her community service included membership on the Iowa City Council and the committee that led to the council-manager form of government. She died in a tragic fire at their home, and later an elementary school was named in her honor.

Philip Jr. ("Gammie," a name we abandoned as soon as he was able to express an opinion) was born in October 1946 while we were living in our first apartment. Wynonna and I soon bought our first home at 209 South Madison, two doors from the home of Haywood Short, and Christine was born there at noon on Christmas day in 1947 and was promptly adorned with bright purple makeup; Michael ("Suki" from the saggy-baggy elephant in one of his favorite books) arrived in January 1949. Beginning in 1947, I taught in the Department of Mechanics and

Hydraulics as a graduate assistant, and received my master's degree in 1949. Richard ("Rikki" for Rikki Tikki Tavi, the mongoose in Kipling's *The Jungle Book*) was born in July 1951, I received my Ph.D. in 1954, and Peter ("Pipper" or P Powerful Pipperinski) was born in July 1955.

Naming the children was not a problem; we wanted to use family names for at least some of them to provide a sense of identity with the past. We quickly decided on Philip for the first one, but considered Alexander (for my father) or Franklin as a middle name because Franklin Roosevelt was fresh in our memory. Wynonna made the final decision to name him Philip Gamaliel Hubbard Jr. Christine's first name was inspired by her arrival on Christmas day; we also considered "Holly." We wanted a name from Wynonna's family for her middle name, and I suggested Marie (Wynonna's middle name), but she gave a resounding *no*! We then easily agreed on Christine Griffin Hubbard. Myke's first name was simply one that we liked, and his middle name was in honor of my late brother Inman, to produce Michael Laurence Hubbard. Names for the next child were chosen from our two grandfathers, Richard Wallace and Charles Griffin, to produce Richard Charles Hubbard. My pet name for Wynonna was Peter, and we decided to immortalize it in naming the last of our children, then added a name that we liked, to produce Peter David Hubbard.

Our lifestyle during this period reflected values from our childhood. Wynonna's family and mine had owned their homes, and we bought our first home at 209 S. Madison Street in 1947. We were unable to get financing from a bank, but Dean Dawson came to our aid once again with the necessary loan at 5 percent simple interest. We managed without an automobile because our house was within a few blocks of work, school, church, and the downtown stores. Some food was purchased at Brady's corner market and brought home in a baby buggy, and large orders were delivered by the larger Economy Grocery. When we had saved sufficient money, we bought a new blue Ford coupe for $1,200 cash in 1950. We could have afforded a more expensive car, but we had better uses for the money. The only options we chose were a heater and two taillights; I bought a radio at wholesale, cut holes where needed, and installed it myself. Our practice was to borrow only for capital expenditures such as a

and lives with her husband Francis Fair in Des Moines. In 1954, Sally Joan Baker joined our family for three years after she graduated from Clarinda High School, and then worked for the university registrar for several years before moving to California. There she was secretary to the dean of the graduate college at the University of California at Berkeley until retiring and founding an award-winning television program, *Wee Poets*, featuring small children of many races. Ruby Ware, an Iowa City native whose family had also housed university students, was the last "nanny" to join the family, and she remained until we bought a new home at 4 West Park Road, next to City Park.

For a few years after moving into our first home, we housed a few members of Kappa Alpha Psi fraternity, painted the basement crimson and cream, and served as the chapter base since they did not have a house. The extended family of "nannies" and fraternity men proved to be a congenial environment for our family, and there was never a shortage of baby-sitters.

As each of our five children was born, he or she was enrolled in the preschool operated by the university. Occasionally, Phil would return from preschool with drawings he had made, and Chris looked forward to the time she would go. The drawings were all that she had seen of preschool, and when her turn came she concentrated on painting to such an extent that we could have papered the living room with her art. Myke was also in the first class of the Parents Cooperative Preschool, which still operates on campus. Health care was provided by the Well-Baby Clinic at the University of Iowa Hospitals and Clinics for regular immunizations and checkups, and we saw doctors in town for some occasions — Dr. Rohrbacher for Phil's birth, the department of obstetrics and gynecology for Chris, and so on. Wynonna has often said that Dr. Spock was a principal consultant during the children's early years. After completing preschool, they all attended the university laboratory elementary and high schools until they were closed in 1972. All but Peter had graduated by then, and he opted for a diploma after completing his junior year. I was the invited speaker at his commencement, which was the last graduating class for the school.

Wynonna and I always managed to attend the children's recitals, plays, football games, and concerts at school because such events were very important to them. Such support was also important to us as parents because that was what we considered to be the norm for family life, not an infringement on our freedom to pursue independent pleasures. In the summer, I frequently sailed Frisbees with the children in the park, and waved at the neighbors as they went by. I was the family barber until crew cuts were no longer fashionable and the boys wanted a decent job.

Walking was a regular feature of our lives during those days: in the week between our wedding and reporting for military duty Wynonna and I explored Iowa City on foot; when we were in State College we hiked out into the mountains; and one of our favorite family vacation spots was the YMCA camp near Estes Park, Colorado, where we became familiar with many of the hiking trails in Rocky Mountain National Park. At home, I took the children to see the flowers in the spring, to the parks, and to explore for fossils in the gravel brought in as fill for the embankment of Interstate Highway 80, then under construction. Phil remembers that I taught them to swim in water too deep for them to touch the bottom of the pool; to this day they love to swim.

Dad thought that bicycles were dangerous and he could not afford to pay for an injury, so I never had one as a child, not even when an old one was offered at no cost. When Phil was around ten years old, I bought bicycles for him, Chris, Myke, and myself, but not for Wynonna; she had never learned to ride a bike. From that day until I was sixty-seven years old, a bicycle became my standard mode of transportation in town. It was especially convenient for moving around the campus quickly, could be parked next to any building, freed the car for others to use, and provided exercise. I rode it year-round except when the streets were slippery with rain or snow, wearing clothing appropriate for the weather. When the children reached the driving age, the inevitable question, "Who gets to use the car?" was answered according to which of us had farthest to go, and who was carrying a load.

The acquisition of an auto opened new recreational horizons for the family, and we often took "triangle" sightseeing trips to nearby communities. The iron triangle went from Iowa City to Mt. Vernon to Cedar Rapids and back home; the silver triangle went from Iowa City to West Liberty to Muscatine and back;

and the golden triangle went from Iowa City to Davenport to Anamosa and home, for example. Wynonna had to learn to drive, and she later said emphatically that wives should not learn to drive from their husbands. I must have been a real ogre. On one trip, we had a flat tire on Rural Highway 6 west of Marengo, and I had begun to change it when a carload of teenage boys stopped. They took over, changed the tire, and put the flat one in the trunk. They waved off our thanks with a cheery "glad to help" and disappeared into the distance.

Phil remembers many details of those early rides: interesting names of towns on the way to Des Moines before Interstate Highway 80 was built, such as Coralville, Tiffin, Oxford, Homestead, Marengo, Grinnell, Newton, and Colfax; on the way back, he knew when we were almost home from the road sound of bricks and the mercury vapor lights as we passed the Veterans' Hospital with the younger ones sound asleep; and trips to little churches in Iowa towns on Race Relations Sundays, where I would be the speaker. He also remembers the smoke-filled house when the stoker-fed furnace acted up; the "spray hoop" or vent for toxic paint fumes in the maintenance shop next door; the four-digit telephone numbers (ours was 3914); eating popcorn in pajamas at the drive-in movie; our three Ford station wagons, the last one a heavy v-8 that he named "the tank"; meeting students and other engineering colleagues — Michel Hug from France, Enzo and Mathilde Macagno from Argentina, and Chia-Shuen Yih from China. He remembers Dean Dawson, and is pleased that his memory will be preserved as one of our "guardian angels."

On one occasion, we invited Rex Carr, a graduate student from Australia, for dinner. Wynonna thought he might appreciate an entree of lamb, a staple of the Australian diet, so she roasted a nice leg of lamb. When it was served, Rex asked, "Where is the outside coating?" She retrieved it from the oven and he ate it with great relish, saying the crusty coating was the best part of the lamb. He also told us of his experience in calling his wife in Australia after he had been away for many months: after a brief conversation, she remarked, "You have an American accent!" (we hadn't noticed). The call went on for perhaps a half hour, and Rex was pleased that they were getting mostly free time: Australian operators informed callers when their three minutes were up, and if they failed to notify the caller, there was no charge for the extra time. He was dismayed to find that American operators had no such obligation; the extra cost of a long call to Australia was substantial.

Our happy life was abruptly interrupted by a tragedy. In November 1951, Mother came to the university hospital for diagnosis of a persistent growth on her neck that had puzzled her Des Moines doctor. She was in good health except for the growth, and we hoped that it was not a cancer. In the course of what we thought was a normal biopsy, the surgeon ruptured her carotid artery and she went into a coma. I sat alone by her side while Paul hurried from Des Moines on a cold and rainy day, but we could only watch helplessly as her life ebbed away. I didn't even have a chance to say "thanks." The Rosa Belle Hubbard student loan fund was established in her memory, but had to be terminated when loans were not repaid.

Our first home had required a lot of maintenance and remodeling, and I bought the necessary tools and supplies to lay new hardwood flooring over the unfinished wide boards, rearrange the kitchen, and install all-new cabinets, sink, refrigerator, freezer, and dishwasher, complete with new wiring and plumbing. At the time, I was on the Iowa City Board of Electrical Examiners, and I asked for an inspection to ensure that I had complied with the relevant construction codes. All our improvements were destroyed when we later sold the house to the city, which cleared the property and sold it to the university as part of the land for the south approach to the university library. Our new house on Park Road was solidly built, and was originally the home of Professor George Bundy Wilson, head of the Department of German. We replaced the old kitchen (twice) and created a family room for a piano and the TV set. One Christmas we splurged and bought a custom-made walnut grandfather clock from the furniture factory at Amana. I still have it in my retirement apartment, but expect that it will be returned to its original location in what is now Peter's home when I no longer need it.

The new home at 4 West Park Road was in an area outside the "red-lined" area (that is, acceptable for occupation by African Americans). We did not buy through a real-estate agent but dealt directly with the owner, James W. Culbertson, a professor of internal medicine, who had come to the university from South Carolina seven years earlier. He was moving to Tennessee, had heard of our difficulties in finding housing, and offered to sell at a very reasonable price. Our new neighbors quickly proved that the reactionary fears of the real-estate establishment were groundless. They welcomed us with open arms, and our children formed close friendships with the neighborhood children. For example, we took Bob Kent, a neighbor's child, as Pete's guest on a vacation to the Rocky Mountains. In contrast to our experience with banks the first time around, when we needed to borrow money to finance the house and then to improve it several times, Clark Houghton, president of the First National Bank, offered to lend us the money on the same terms as a GI loan. Although I had not known him when he and I entered the university as freshmen in 1940, we have become good friends through our activities in the church and the community. In 1988, Wynonna and I sold the home to Peter and Mary and moved into a comfortable two-bedroom apartment in Montclair Park on First Avenue, leaving many household furnishings and part of our book collection with Peter and Mary.

I was somewhat disappointed by Wynonna's decision not to return to college after I entered the army, but I didn't urge her to continue because she had never indicated any desire for a career other than marriage. Although she had no personal plans, she supported the feminist goals for equality of opportunity and reward for work, as she indicated in an interview by Barbara Yost for the *Daily Iowan*, published on March 15, 1972.

> One issue Ms. Hubbard is involved in is women's liberation. "I think it's great," she said. "I particularly agree with equal employment and equal pay for equal jobs. I think the other things are more personal and have to be worked out within the marriage. You can't have a certain rule that applies to everyone."
>
> She does go along with the new abbreviation "Ms." "It's fine," she said. . . .
>
> In their years at Iowa, there have been many memorable

moments on campus for the Hubbards, but probably the time she will remember most is the day of the Carver contribution to the University [Roy and Lucille Carver of Muscatine, generous benefactors who supported health care, the Museum of Art, the Educational Opportunity Program, faculty professorships, athletics, and other programs to enhance the quality of the university].

"I could forget about the riots," she said, "but I think this year the most memorable occasion was when we got the Carver contribution. They're gracious people. You'd think that people with that much money would be a little hard to know, but they're not."

Although we were partners in happily nurturing a family of five active children, each of us had pursuits that involved the other only indirectly. I was deeply involved in university and community responsibilities in which Wynonna showed very little interest, while she managed to assume an increasing schedule of community and civic activities in which I was not involved. In the early years, she supported the United Methodist Women and helped in Scout and Pony Club activities. As the children demanded less and less of her time, she joined and participated in the International Club, a women's organization that hosted events for students from abroad and supported cooperative programs involving people from other countries. She also worked regularly with the Nineteenth Century Club, a local women's organization devoted to mutual educational development.

For many years, Wynonna was a volunteer worker for both the Mercy and university hospitals. At Mercy, she worked in the gift shop and for several years she was also on the hospital board of directors; at the university hospital, she worked in the library. I was especially grateful for the many letters of condolence from her coworkers in both hospitals after her death.

Her interest in the welfare of juveniles was reflected in her service as a member of the board of directors of Families, Inc., a six-county agency that held its regular meetings in West Branch. The agency provided juvenile offenders and their families with necessary counseling and guidance while permitting the juveniles to continue living at home. I thought it was an excellent concept, and Wynonna derived a great deal of satisfaction from the work. Since she preferred not to drive on the highway, a fellow board member always provided transportation.

After serving a three-year term on the Iowa City Civil Service Commission, Wynonna was elected in 1975 to chair the commission for a second term. The commission's primary function was to examine and certify candidates for police officers and firefighters in Iowa City. Christine's husband, Jim Walters, was one of the applicants for firefighter, and he passed with flying colors but decided to take another job. While she was chair, the commission examined Linda Eaton, whose candidacy was controversial because no woman had ever served as a firefighter and many people, including some of the current firefighters, thought they never should. Eaton passed all of the requirements easily, and was duly employed. The controversy did not end there, because she proceeded to nurse her baby in the station house during breaks from duty and filed a complaint against her colleagues for harassment. Although Wynonna was not particularly comfortable with controversy, she handled the acrimony very well and continued her work with several organizations at all times.

Wynonna had trouble telling jokes because she laughed so hard that she cried before reaching the punch line. She enjoyed reading, with a distinct preference for mysteries, especially those by Agatha Christie. We read to each other, and that became especially important during the many periods when she was disabled. Mealtimes were special, and we made a point of all eating together, followed by long discussions led by Wynonna. Visits by her father were especially welcome — he made delicious dinner rolls without ever measuring anything. She often prepared gourmet meals, and had a large collection of recipe books and *Gourmet* magazines that I eventually donated to the Iowa City Public Library, together with boxes of her mysteries. More boxes of books by and about women were donated to the public library and the Women's Action and Resource Center. A friend recently told me that Wynonna's name was in the front of the book *Alaska* by James Michener that he had borrowed from the library.

We had widely divergent views on clothing. I didn't like

shopping for anything, especially clothes, so that my really decent clothes were gifts from Wynonna and the children. In contrast, she enjoyed shopping in general, and especially for wearing apparel. According to our friends, her taste was excellent, and they looked forward to seeing what she would wear on various occasions. Although I paid no attention to her clothing budget, she was quite judicious, and I suspected that she sometimes bought me something to wear to ease her conscience. I was her particular despair because I failed to notice when she wore something new. I escaped by telling her the truth: "When I look into your eyes, I see only you, and don't notice whether you are wearing a formal gown or a gunnysack." She would give me a knowing look and respond, "You charlatan!" but her voice was softer. Discretion is sometimes the better part of valor. On another occasion, she collapsed in laughter in spite of a bad cold when I lovingly murmured, "Your eyes look like pieces of liver in bowls of tomato soup."

I was also a source of despair in the matter of weight control. When she went on a crash diet, I ate the same thing so that she wouldn't have to prepare regular meals for me, which might tempt her to backslide. She sighed in resignation when the pounds quickly drained from my frame while she slowly edged downward. Once, when she was worrying about her weight, she commented that she didn't want to be like the storybook woman who was six ax handles wide. When we saw an exceptionally obese person walking in tight clothing without a girdle, she said it reminded her of two cats fighting in a gunnysack. Thereafter, a simple reference to liver in tomato soup, six ax handles, or cats in a gunnysack inspired a round of laughter — our private cryptic jokes.

As we expected, our family of five active children kept us busy. The boys played Little League baseball and became Eagle Scouts, and when no mothers were available for a Cub Scout den, another father and I obtained permission from Boy Scout headquarters to serve as den fathers. Chris took dance lessons at the university and joined the Pony Club, where she rode and cared for Mr. Good, her pony with a white mane and white socks. I spent some frigid days helping the owner, Betsy Coester, build more stables, and Chris suffered frostbite. Our memories are not frostbitten, however.

Soon after we moved into our home on Park Road, Phil began delivering the *Des Moines Register*, and the route became a Hubbard family monopoly as Myke, Rick, and Pete followed. (That has continued into the next generation — Peter's son Robert carried the same route.) Their beagle went along as they delivered papers, and often returned in the otherwise empty delivery bag on bitterly cold winter mornings. Chris handed out baskets at the nearby swimming pool, and later worked as an assistant at a reducing salon "fat farm," where she was impressed by severely overweight patrons who removed their rings to "lose" weight before weighing in. While he was in college, Phil worked as a salesman in Hands Jewelry store; Myke worked on a construction crew, where he became streamlined with rippling muscles, and was a research assistant in the social sciences laboratory as an undergraduate; Rick worked with a painting crew when he returned from Harvard for the summer; after graduating from high school, Pete worked as a general office assistant for the architect/contractor Powers Willis Associates. As far as I can recall, none of the children ever received an allowance. When they went to college, we provided a subsidy for educational expenses, but gave it to them to manage, rather than having college bills sent to us for payment.

Through several colleagues in the university, I had direct contact with the Quaker (Friends) community, which is quite strong in Iowa. Pres. Herbert Hoover, a native of nearby West Branch, was a Quaker, as are many of the farmers in that area today. I visited in their homes, especially that of Verlin Pemberton, whose daughter Beulah married Clark de Haven, one of my student colleagues in engineering. I went to services in both the annual and the four-year Quaker churches, and spoke to the congregation at one service. The Friends operated Scattergood, a boarding high school in which the students had substantial responsibilities for operating the surrounding farm and the programs of the school under the splendid direction of Leonora Goodenow. Wynonna and I would have been pleased to enroll our children there, but finally decided to leave them in the university school they had attended since preschool.

Our social life revolved around the children, and the parents of their classmates became some of our closest friends. When I later worked with those parents in connection with my administrative work, there was a level of understanding and trust that enabled us to carry out our work smoothly and quickly. Sam Becker's daughter Judy was Rick's classmate, and John Gerber's daughter Ann was Chris's friend. Mike Spriestersbach was best man at Phil's wedding, and his sister Ann was in Chris's class. Jean Kendall's daughter Debbie was a classmate of Peter. John and Sam provided invaluable support in my work for the Iowa Center for the Arts, Spriestersbach became my fellow vice president, and I appointed Jean director of Iowa Memorial Union.

When I lived in Des Moines, I never had a pet, but Wynonna had a cat named Bathsheba. As soon as we had a home of our own, we had a long succession of pets, beginning with Hubba Hubba, a certified mutt who liked mashed potatoes. Lester Q. Trawver was a white boxer whose parents were registered, but we got him at a bargain price because boxers can be registered only if they are mostly brown or black. When I decided to dispose of him after he chewed up the children's encyclopedia, I remembered an item in the old *Liberty* magazine. A company had a trainload of white salmon that was not marketable because the public preferred pink salmon. When they advertised "genuine white salmon, guaranteed not to turn pink," they soon sold the entire inventory. I advertised in the *Iowa City Press Citizen* want ads "genuine white boxer, guaranteed not to turn brown" and we found a happy buyer. His successors included Alfred T. Brewster, an uncertified cross-bred retriever; Wiggles, who was especially good at retrieving hot dogs; and Alice, a purebred cocker spaniel. We made trips to Fountain Falls, a pet shop on old Rohret Road, and obtained a variety of goldfish and Sherwood, a guinea pig of undetermined gender (Pete commented that only another guinea pig would care) who was named for the stereo equipment we bought at the same time. Christine's favorite cat Peanuts was blinded in one eye by a big orange cat that was the neighborhood bully, and she disappeared for a long time until we found her cowering under the porch. People admired the multicolored eye, not realizing that it was blind.

After a long succession of dogs, cats, guinea pigs, hamsters, and goldfish, we drove to West Des Moines and bought a beagle from Wynonna's childhood neighbors, Charlie and Irene Swink. Charlie raised beagles for hunting, and the Swinks had a kennel in their yard, surrounded by a fence that created a runway around the building. We had the pick of the litter, and quickly learned to love Huckleberry. Everyone was shocked when he was trapped by high ridges of snow in our driveway and I unknowingly backed the car over him. We immediately drove to West Des Moines to get another pup from the same litter, and returned with Cleo. We were puzzled when she never left the yard, circling the house as if it was surrounded by a fence, until we realized that she had developed the habit when confined by the kennel fence in West Des Moines. She quickly became a member of the family, but her hunting instinct often led her somewhat astray. There was no leash law at the time, and when we could hear her distant howling in the nearby park, we knew that she was on the trail of a rabbit. She was spoiled and overate grossly when the participants in our annual African American family pig roast took turns feeding her. It turned out to be too much for her aging heart, and she died at the ripe old age of sixteen.

We traveled frequently when the children were growing, and our experiences illustrate the climate of the times and the way our family was developing. When I grew up in Des Moines, there was no travel as a family except for a rare trip to Ledges State Park near Boone, when a generous neighbor invited us to go along on a one-day trip. The situation was very different in the next generation, and we traveled throughout the United States and Canada. I can recall some of the more memorable trips. Around 1969, our family traveled to Florida and Grand Bahama with the University of Iowa Alumni Association trip, which included a game with Miami University in the Orange Bowl (not the postseason bowl game). Family reunions were anticipated with pleasure, and were held in Iowa City, Association Camp in the Colorado Rockies, and Washington, D.C. (and Grand Cayman, British West Indies, after Wynonna had died).

My grandson Anthony and I had an interesting experience prior to a family reunion in Washington, D.C., when he was nine years old. He had traveled alone from Seattle to spend a week with us in Iowa City, changing planes in Minneapolis en route to Cedar Rapids, where I met the plane. I had to wait until all other passengers had deplaned, then went aboard, identified myself, and drove to Iowa City. For the trip, the airline gave him a large badge marked "Unaccompanied Child," and he kept it as a souvenir. A week later the two of us flew to Washington via Detroit for the reunion. I noticed that the cabin attendants eyed us carefully, but I didn't know why until we stopped to change planes. As we emerged from the plane, airport security personnel called us aside and asked me for identification. Anthony had been wearing his souvenir badge, and they wanted to know why I was obviously escorting an "unaccompanied child." They did not immediately accept my explanation, but asked us to remain where they could watch us until the next flight arrived. I thanked them for being alert to possible danger for Anthony, and we completed the trip without further incident.

Our preparations for vacations were rather unusual because Wynonna depended on the rest of the family for ideas for destinations, routes, reading a map, where to stop or eat, and play. She prepared the clothing and snacks for the journey, but once we were under way she left the daily decisions up to others and relaxed to enjoy a well-earned vacation. After the first trip to the Rockies, we played a game to see who would be the first to see the mountains on the distant horizon after we left Highway 25 and were heading west on Highway 34. False sightings disqualified the guesser, and the winner got to choose an extra-special treat when we stopped for ice-cream cones. We also looked forward to the rapidly cooling air on the westward drive through the canyon of the Big Thompson River en route to Estes Park and on to the YMCA camp at an altitude of 8,000 feet.

Racism often cast a pall on our pleasure whenever we had to stop for the night. We were sometimes exhausted from driving for hours trying to find a motel that would accommodate a black family. Phil remembers standing behind me in the car, helping to keep me awake as we drove for many miles in Pennsylvania trying to locate a place to spend the night. In preparing for one trip, I wrote to an AAA-approved motel in Grand Island, Nebraska, to reserve accommodations, and got a written confirmation. When we appeared, the manager refused to honor the reservation because it seems I had forgotten to tell them that we were not white. His assistant, mortified by his action, phoned around and located the Rodeo Motel, which accommodated us with pleasure. I wrote a complaint to the Grand Island Chamber of Commerce and received an apologetic response, and of course we thereafter gave our business to the Rodeo Motel. We encountered similar problems in other locations, but not in our several trips through Canada. Our American experience was not an unbroken story of rejection, however: when we stopped for dinner at a restaurant west of Minneapolis, a complete stranger picked up the tab for our family of seven, commenting that we were a very attractive family. When we stopped for a picnic in the North Platte city park, a couple went out of their way to introduce themselves and gave us a basket of home-fried chicken. We never camped out; our idea of "roughing it" was to spend the night at a motel with only black-and-white TV. On the whole, we enjoyed our travels, saw many beautiful places, and met enough friendly and gracious people that we always anticipated vacation travel with pleasure.

We spent several of our vacations in Rocky Mountain National Park, staying at the YMCA Association Camp near Estes Park. We walked many of the hiking trails in the park, and one hike in particular remains in my memory. Wynonna did not feel well because of the altitude, so she and Chris stayed at our cabin while Phil, Myke, Rick, Pete, and I went to the 10,000-foot Twin Sisters peak at the eastern edge of the Rockies. We climbed through the pine forest to the top, then to a ranger fire lookout station on a high platform. We could look to the west and see several ranges of the magnificent Rockies; looking to the east, we saw the Great Plains stretching to the horizon. I had brought a Bible for the occasion, and from that vantage point read one of my favorite poems, the Eighth Psalm, verses 3/9:

When I look at thy heavens, the work of thy fingers, the moon and the stars which thou hast established;

What is man that thou art mindful of him, and the son of man that thou dost care for him?

Yet thou hast made him little less than God, and dost crown him with glory and honor.

Thou hast given him dominion over the works of thy hands; thou hast put all things under his feet, all sheep and oxen and also the beasts of the field, the birds of the air, and the fish of the sea, whatever passes along the paths of the sea.

Oh Lord, our Lord, how majestic is thy name in all the earth!

As I review my life in its twilight, I am impressed by two themes that have arisen time and again: the centrality of family and a reverence for humankind, individually and collectively. With regard to the latter, my ideas represent a lifetime of immersion in the Christian ethic and I am acquainted with the official Methodist doctrine, even teaching Sunday school using materials from the Methodist Publishing House. Religion involves faith and belief at least as much as understanding, and an insistence on complete understanding as a condition of acceptance erases the line between religion and worldly philosophies. My beliefs were absorbed with Mother's milk, and will remain with me to the end. I must confess, however, that I do not comprehend complicated theology, especially some of the ideas that come through the mass media. I have concluded that I think in terms that are too simple, because I can summarize the essential core of my belief in three passages from the first three books of the Pentateuch.

(1) God is defined in the first chapter of Genesis, verse 27. "And God created the human in his image, in the image of God He created him; Male and female He created them."

(2) In the nineteenth chapter of Exodus, verse 3: "You shall have no other gods before me."

(3) From Leviticus, chapter 19, verse 18: "You shall not take vengeance or bear any grudge against the sons of your own people, but you shall love your neighbor as yourself: I am the Lord."

In the Sermon on the Mount (Matthew 22:37–40), Jesus combines these laws: "You shall love the Lord your God with all your heart, and with all your soul, and with all your mind. This is the first and greatest commandment.

"And a second is like it, You shall love your neighbor as yourself. On these two commandments depend all the law and the prophets."

From the Genesis passage, the logic principle of symmetry —

if A equals B, then B equals A — tells me that God is collective humankind. The unique supremacy of God is stated in the passage from Exodus, but I believe that the concept is diluted by the symbolism of the concept of the Holy Trinity and related doctrines.

The definition of *neighbor* in the Matthew passage is clarified in the tenth chapter of Luke, verses 29–37:

> But he [a lawyer], desiring to justify himself, said to Jesus "and who is my neighbor?" Jesus replied "A man was going down from Jerusalem to Jericho, and he fell among robbers, who stripped him and beat him, and departed, leaving him half-dead. Now by chance a priest was going down that road; and when he saw him he passed by on the other side. So likewise a Levite, when came to the place and saw him, passed by on the other side. But a Samaritan, as he journeyed, came to where he was; and when he saw him, he had compassion, and went to him and bound up his wounds, pouring on oil and wine; then he set him on his own beast and brought him to an inn, and took care of him. And the next day he took out two denarii and gave them to the innkeeper, saying 'take care of him; and whatever more you spend, I will repay you when I come back.' Which of these three, do you think, proved neighbor to the man who fell among the robbers?" He said, "the one who showed mercy on him." And Jesus said to him "go and do likewise."

The full meaning of this passage is better understood by noting that the Judeans and the Samaritans had been mortal enemies for 700 years; even the shadow of a Samaritan falling on a pregnant woman was believed to cause a miscarriage. By using this example, Jesus made it clear that all humankind are neighbors to each other without distinction of race or tribe; there should be no enemies.

The meaning of *love* in the above passage may not be clear to everyone because there are three words in the Greek of the New Testament for which English has only a single word. Martin Luther King's scholarly explanation can help at this point: *eros* refers to an aesthetic or romantic love, and anticipates a personal pleasure; *philia* denotes a reciprocal emotion in which one loves because he is loved, and it is important in building a spirit of community. When Jesus commands, "Love your neigh-bor," he refers to the third word in the Greek: *agape* — the spirit of God dwelling in the human heart. Agape anticipates no reward or personal satisfaction, and it does not depend on a reciprocal action. It is a redeeming goodwill for all humans, purely spontaneous, unmotivated, groundless, and creative. It does not discriminate between worthy and unworthy people or depend on any qualities they might possess. If the object of my love responds with spite and hatred, I do not withdraw my love because I cannot; I am responding to a higher command from which there can be no retreat. I can have no enemies, and I *must* respond to human need. That is the ideal.

Human beings are not perfect, and one cannot infallibly meet the severe demands of the command to love. The concept of atonement enters at this point: if one repents after straying and does not repeat the error, then it should not be necessary to carry an eternal burden of remorse. This rather simplistic description of atonement illustrates my introductory admission, that I do not comprehend complicated theology. Nonetheless, the three passages have been a polestar to guide my decisions. Although I often stray, that star can be used to correct my course. I should emphasize that my religious beliefs are a guide for my personal behavior and my teaching, not a weapon to impose my will on others or a standard to judge their actions. If this essay on religion reads like a sermon, so be it.

Many people reject religious beliefs as a form of superstition or because religion has been used to justify bigotry, greed, and violence. One can find convincing evidence to support these criticisms, since there is a long tradition of translating the basic principles of various religions into contradictory doctrines that support earthly ambitions. Even people who agree with these criticisms, however, can appreciate the works of fine art that have been inspired by sincere believers. Our world has been enriched immeasurably by the art, architecture, drama, music, and poetry that have been created to express religious beliefs transcending temporal concerns.

Two of my favorite prayers may help to illustrate how religion is an integral part of my life.

Peter Marshall, longtime chaplain of the U.S. Senate, often used this morning prayer: "Give me the *strength* to change those things that should be changed, the *patience* to accept those things I cannot change, and the *wisdom* to know which is which."

With reference to *strength*, I prefer action as opposed to a passive reliance on divine intervention, and the use of a guiding philosophy to avoid a rudderless wandering like a bull in a china shop. My guide is the polestar identified above — the welfare of humankind.

My favorite evening prayer recognizes human fallibility and the need for contrition.

> If I have wounded any soul today
> If I have caused one foot to go astray
> If I have walked in mine own willful way,
> Dear Lord, forgive.
> Forgive the sins I have confessed to thee
> Forgive my secret sins I do not see
> Oh guide me, help me, and my keeper be
> Dear Lord, Amen.

As our family life pursued its course, the children began to graduate from high school. As each one headed for college, I accompanied them (except for Myke's trip to Uganda) to visit the prospective campus, learning more about the variety of institutions. When the college years began, I started an informal record of the aggregate numbers of years the children had studied. I eventually stopped counting after the number had reached thirty-eight.

Philip enrolled in the University of Iowa in 1965 and obtained his B.S. in 1969 with a major in anthropology. Along the way he spent one semester and one summer in Mexico. He went on to earn the J.D. from the University of Michigan Law School in 1972, pursued a diverse career in law in Seattle, and was elected judge of Superior Court in King County, Washington, in 1996.

Christine decided to study at American University in Washington, D.C., so we visited the campus and she enrolled in 1966. She transferred to Iowa the next year, and obtained the B.G.S. degree in 1970. She took advanced work in Chinese for two summers at Middlebury College in Vermont, and later enrolled for graduate work at the University of Iowa, earning the M.A.

in library and information science in 1990. She is now a reference librarian in the university library.

When Michael graduated from high school, his best friend Dan Norton was planning to accompany his family to Uganda where Dan's father, Professor Dee Norton, had a one-year appointment. They invited Myke to go with them, and he enrolled at Makerere University College in Kampala for the 1967–1968 academic year. He transferred to the University of Iowa, graduating in 1971 with a B.S. in psychology, then continued his studies at Stanford University, where he earned the Ph.D. in psychology, and later obtained a Master of Biostatistics degree from Columbia University. Since 1984, he has conducted research at Research Triangle Institute in Durham, North Carolina, as a psychologist-statistician.

Richard received a scholarship to Harvard University in 1969, and earned the A.B. degree magna cum laude in 1973 with a major in government. In his work with the Phillips Brooks House, he "adopted" a little brother, Keith, who negotiated the subway system from South Boston to Cambridge to attend Rick's commencement ceremony. Richard continued at Harvard Medical School, receiving his M.D. in 1977. He conducted research at the National Heart, Lung and Blood Institute for seven years, then cast his lot with industry, where he is executive director of clinical research for the Searle division of Monsanto in Skokie, Illinois.

Peter was caught with one year to go when the University High School was closed in 1972, and elected to receive a diploma instead of transferring to West High. He enrolled at the University of Iowa, earning the B.S. in 1976 with a major in history. He continued his education at the University of Wisconsin–Madison, and received the Ph.D. with a major in medieval history. He always loved his home in Iowa City, and now lives in the house where he grew up, while serving as assistant to the dean of the College of Liberal Arts.

Selecting a life partner is perhaps the most important decision one must make, and we informed our children that they were free to make the choice without any restrictions, except that they might introduce us to their intended (of course, they did). Once they made a choice, however, their chosen spouse would be a full member of the family — no second-class people, no stepchildren, or other hyphenated designations. We occasionally worried that they would be restricted during the high school years by the virtual absence of African American contemporaries for dating, but they managed quite well with their longtime friends and classmates. We were especially relieved when they met new friends in college and graduate school. Wynonna and I watched with increasing puzzlement as none of the children chose African American spouses and the family became a virtual genealogical rainbow: their choices of spouses justified our faith in their judgment, and in the final analysis, we thought that everything turned out very well.

Philip Jr. married Susan Beth Bale, and their children Anthony and Monica have been delighted to learn that their Russian ancestors included saddle makers for the czars who communicated in Yiddish at their home near Vilnius.

Christine's husband, James P. Walters, is the son of Iowa teachers and sheep farmers; his mother was of English descent, and his father's family migrated from the Ukraine. Their chosen son Matthew is now the only member of the family with strictly African ancestry.

Michael married Carol Clark Torres, whose son Peter Joseph brings an English, Irish, and Puerto Rican ancestry to the family. Their chosen daughter Sarah reflects the European and African ancestry of the rest of the family, plus some American Indian forebears. Sarah was baptized in the Roman Catholic Church of her mother, and Myke has joined them as a member.

When Richard and Alaka traveled to India, their children Shanti and Eric were enchanted by the experience of seeing their great-grandmother, who still lives in Ujjain, Madya Pradesh, where their mother and grandmother were also born. They also visited cousins, aunts, and uncles in Pune (Poona), near the birthplace of their grandfather.

Peter's wife, Mary Kay Meyer, is the daughter of a farmer and a nurse in northeast Iowa whose ancestors migrated to Iowa from Germany and Switzerland. Their children Robert (named for Wynonna's brother), Neil, and Katherine are frequent visitors to Postville, Iowa, and are well known and loved by their German Lutheran relatives.

No one could have possibly planned such a remarkable diversification of the family genealogy in one generation, but the delightful result is a congenial family from Seattle to North Carolina that enjoys vacations together and is well prepared for an increasingly diverse world in the twenty-first century. All of them are following successful professional careers, and their children are happy and well adjusted. I find it interesting that all of them are homeowners in university communities: Phil near the university area of Seattle, Chris and Peter in Iowa City, Myke in Chapel Hill, North Carolina, and Rick in Evanston, Illinois. Most gratifying of all, in a period of shocking divorce statistics they have established stable, enduring family relationships just as Wynonna and I did.

On Election Day 1996, I traveled to Seattle to join Phil and his family in watching the election returns after a spirited campaign. I returned on January 21, and cannot forget the thrill of seeing him introduced by his colleague Christine Gregoire, attorney general for the state of Washington, to be installed as Superior Court judge Philip G. Hubbard Jr. in the King County courthouse. We wished that Wynonna could have shared the occasion.

As each of our grandchildren was born, we invested a small but significant sum in growth securities, to be used when they completed high school and considered college or prepared for a vocation. Our oldest grandchild, Anthony, has now received an associate degree in culinary arts at Johnson and Wales University in Rhode Island and has entered a career as a chef. The next oldest, Matthew, graduated from West High School in Iowa City and plans to enroll in Coe College in the fall of 1998. Monica will graduate at the same time, and has decided to attend Bennington College in Vermont. Stay tuned for a continuing report as seven more grandchildren proceed through the educational systems of Iowa City, Evanston, and Chapel Hill.

How does one leave a mark for future generations? Some leaders, such as Moses, Gandhi, and Lincoln, did so through their own actions. A few great teachers such as Jesus have left their legacy through their disciples and others whose lives they touched. Most of us must rely on our descendants, or we disturb hardly a grain in the sands of time. Only time will provide the answer.

All of our children have found opportunities to travel to other countries, apart from the family trips described above:

Phil spent a summer in Mérida, Mexico, as an exchange student in Iowa's sister state of Yucatán, plus a semester in Teotihuacán, excavating artifacts with an anthropology class. Chris and her husband Jim spent several weeks hiking through the mountains of Nepal and Sikkim. Myke spent his freshman year at Makerere University in Uganda. Rick went to Colombia for one of his medical school rotations, and then spent a year in tropical medicine research at Gorgas Memorial Laboratory in Panama while Alaka was conducting her dissertation research on the impact of a massive hydroelectric development project on the indigenous Cuna Indians. Peter and Mary spent a year in Germany while collecting materials for his doctoral research in medieval history.

When I was selected for a second Fulbright-Hays scholarship in 1968, Wynonna, Philip, Richard, and Peter accompanied me on my lecture tour at the principal universities in Venezuela, Brazil, Uruguay, Argentina, Chile, Peru, and Ecuador. Christine and Michael did not accompany us because Myke was spending his freshman year in Uganda, and Chris was reluctant to leave her boyfriend James Walters, who later became her husband. Phil was curious about the expense of the trip, and asked me how much it would cost. When I told him, he said, "That's enough to buy a Cadillac!" I then asked, "Would you rather have a Cadillac?" The immediate answer from all of them was a resounding "No!"

Most of our time was spent in Uruguay, where I conducted research in the College of Engineering at National University. The mail service in Montevideo was quite unreliable; if the address was not exact in all details, the letter might not be delivered under circumstances that would be easily handled in many countries. To demonstrate the difference, I sent a letter to my secretary addressed simply: Hubbard, 52242, USA, knowing that the university had a unique zip code and I was the only Hubbard in the university at that time. It was promptly delivered to my secretary.

Our departure from Quito was especially interesting. The owner of our hotel, a graduate of the Michigan State program in hotel management, had converted a mansion into an elegant guest house, and he recommended that we skip the first leg of our flight home and take a scenic bus trip to the port city of

Guayaquil. There we could meet our international flight — the plane had to refuel because it could not take off with a full load in the rarefied air of Quito. We took his advice, and the spectacular ride on the Ruta de Las Condores took us through a pass over the roof of the Andes where there was no tree line — in that equatorial climate, trees grew all the way to the top of mountains reaching 19,000 feet. We looked down on the clouds far below, saw sloths in their natural habitats, ate lunch on the moving bus, and bought bananas and trinkets from children at bus stops. The hotel owner had warned us that Guayaquil was a lusty city where we should be careful and not walk around the streets, so we were not surprised when the driver of our taxi to the airport had to stop and disperse some men who were trying to steal our luggage from the rack on top.

In all cases, we had adequate time to take side trips to points of interest in the surrounding territory: a giant soccer stadium in São Paolo, Punta del Este in Uruguay, mountain resorts in Chile, a limousine ride with an enterprising owner to view Inca ruins in Peru, standing astride the equator in Ecuador, and many other places.

Political conditions in Uruguay and Argentina in 1968 were in sharp contrast with those in 1962 when Argentina was a seething cauldron of protest activity. Uruguay, on the other hand, was extolled as a model of peaceful democratic rule with its "colegio" system, in which a quartet of men ruled as a committee with the chairmanship rotating among them every four years; the president's official residence was essentially a museum. Six years later, anti-American sentiment ran high, and riots in the Avenida Independencia were common, but the university campus was honored by the police as a sanctuary that they would not enter. When I went downtown despite a general warning from the Fulbright representative, I was affected by tear gas from a canister that had just killed a bystander after being ejected from a launcher. We hired a local student to tutor our children in Spanish, and when she later visited us in Iowa City, she was appalled to see uniformed troopers on the University of Iowa campus during the protest movement around 1969, saying that would not happen in Uruguay. The turmoil seemed to be limited to Montevideo, because when we were on a bus en route to the port for the Aliscafo (hydrofoil) to Buenos

Aires, a passenger with a beautiful tenor voice spontaneously serenaded his traveling colleagues with a rendition of the aria "O solo mio." That was reminiscent of my undergraduate days when Conrad Schadt, a graduate student from Williamsburg, Iowa, would serenade us with arias from Gilbert and Sullivan and other operas while we were conducting research in the hydraulics laboratory.

In 1976, I was selected (after ten years as dean of academic affairs) by the National Science Foundation to join a U.S. delegation to a UNESCO conference in New Delhi on the education and training of engineers and technologists. Wynonna accompanied me, and we spent two days in London en route to the meeting, and an additional two days in Rome on the way home. En route from Frankfort to Delhi, we spent a long night in the plane at Teheran because the flight bypassed Beirut owing to the continuing warfare there. Wynonna loved the yogurt in Teheran, and asked for an extra bottle for later consumption. She consumed the contents, but Mary remembers seeing the bottle, which Wynonna kept as a souvenir. The professional meeting was productive, and we enjoyed the warm hospitality of our Indian hosts for two weeks.

After the conference, we remained as tourists and visited Agra and Jaipur in central India, then traveled to Kashmir for a few days. Living in a houseboat on Dal Lake was a memorable experience, with our own cook and a boatman to shuttle us back and forth. The houseboats had been constructed by the British because the Moguls refused to sell their land. The Moguls built a road on an embankment across the middle of the lake to move their troops. With different types of gardens at seven locations around it, Dal Lake is known as "the most beautiful lake in the world." Salesmen with different kinds of merchandise came to the houseboat by rowboat; one boat, filled with fresh iridescent red-gold saffron, showed me for the first time what was meant in stories about monks in "saffron-hued robes." We also went by hired auto to Gul Marg, a beautiful meadow of flowers emerging from the snow in the Himalayan spring. The driver was cautious because we were near an area of dispute between India and Pakistan.

During our stay in Italy on the way home, we took a bus

from Rome along the coast to Naples and Pompeii and from there across the Bay of Naples by hydrofoil to the Isle of Capri. After lunch in a charming restaurant on top of the mountain, we returned to the harbor and on by rowboat to the Blue Grotto. The entrance to the grotto was so low that we had to duck our heads, and once inside, the reason for the name was evident. Light entered primarily through the water, bathing the interior in beautiful azure. To complete the romantic picture, the boatmen sang "Santa Lucia" in beautiful tenor voices. It was a great trip for a second honeymoon, except that we never had a first one!

My last trip abroad with Wynonna was a 1988 cruise on the Danube sponsored by the University of Iowa Foundation. With 123 other tourists from the United States, we flew to Istanbul and spent three days exploring the cities on both sides of the Bosporus, then took a stormy cruise across the Black Sea to the mouth of the Danube. There we transferred to a river cruiser, MS *Ukraina*, sailing under the Soviet flag. For the next two weeks, we traveled upstream to Passau, stopping along the way at Bucharest (via a short bus ride), Belgrade, Budapest, the Iron Gate, Bratislava, and Vienna. From Passau we went by bus over the autobahns to Munich.

Wynonna and I occasionally commented when problems arose, "No one ever promised us a rose garden," and we believed that in general our fortune was good. Not perfect, however: Wynonna suffered a severe attack of pericarditis in fall 1959, had recurrent episodes of complications from a rheumatoid factor, and spent many months in the hospital through the next thirty years. Our many friends gathered around during those occasions, bringing large quantities of soup and saffron bread, for example. The children responded magnificently and demonstrated an ability to assume responsibility that we had never suspected. We employed a very competent housekeeper, Mrs. Hostetler from Kalona, who kept the house in good order, did the laundry, and helped with the cooking. From time to time, we employed other women from Kalona and Wellman, and went to the wedding when one of them was married in the Mennonite church near Wellman. We also employed Inez Foster, an African American who had long lived in Iowa City.

Before moving away, she transplanted many varieties of perennial flowers from her home between Ralston Creek and Dubuque Street to various places in our yard.

There were long periods when Wynonna bravely carried on, and I assumed that she would outlive me and made financial arrangements accordingly. It was not to be, however: when I took her to the hospital in winter 1990, the doctors informed me that she could not survive yet another time. The unthinkable was about to happen, but I was able to tell her "thanks." All of our children with their spouses and children were on hand when we were informed at 10:52 P.M. on March 3, 1990, that Wynonna had breathed her last tortured breath after spending two weeks on a ventilator in the ICU.

Shortly after her death, more than 150 friends and colleagues contributed to the Wynonna G. Hubbard Scholarship that had been suggested by our children. Each year, the fully endowed scholarship is awarded to an African American undergraduate woman at the university who is designated by the provost in recognition of her contribution to the well-being of others.

The first recipient, Marci Cannon of Toledo, Ohio, was an excellent scholar who majored in journalism and sociology and graduated in 1993. She was an officer in black student organizations on campus, wrote for the *New Challenger*, a student publication, sang with the Voices of Soul choir, served as a peer assistant, and was executive assistant for Substance Abuse Services, Inc. in her hometown. Marci returned to the university after doing community work in her hometown, finished law school, served as assistant attorney general of the state of Ohio, and now practices law in Kansas City.

The second recipient, Traevena Potter-Hall of Cedar Rapids, also established an outstanding record as a student. She assisted Pres. Hunter Rawlings and members of his administration in improving the campus environment, and was a splendid role model in her own right. She served an internship in Washington, D.C., and planned to seek degrees in law and African American studies after graduating in 1994. Traevena enrolled in law school as planned, and now is director of top scholar recruitment in the office of admissions while her husband completes work on his doctorate.

In spring 1995, Jeanne Pugh of Ames, Iowa, was selected to

receive the scholarship. While she maintained an excellent academic record majoring in global studies and prelaw, Jeanne served as an officer in the Associated Iowa Honors Students, as an orientation adviser in 1993 and 1994, and as an undergraduate member of the Historical Perspective evaluating committee. She planned to pursue a career in law.

Willene Owens, the 1996 recipient, was a sophomore from Davenport who majored in journalism and mass communications with a minor in speech pathology and theater. Her perfect academic record placed her on the dean's list each semester, even though she carried a larger than average schedule of courses. Her activities include part-time librarian at the Hardin medical library, journalism intern at the *Quad City Times*, broadcasting intern at St. Ambrose University, mentor in the DARE program, NAACP Youth Award for Community Service (1995), and news writer for her local church.

Rahni Spencer received the 1997 award on the basis of her excellent record: she was an Opportunity at Iowa scholar with double honors majors in film and theater, the president of her floor in Burge Hall, and was selected for the dean's list in the College of Liberal Arts. She maintained a busy schedule of activities related to her academic majors and Latin American dance, and was cited for teaching multicultural education in the public schools. Her volunteer service included the Museum of Natural History and public access television.

Wynonna's death was especially shocking because, in my characteristic, overoptimistic way, I had assumed that she would outlive me. Her life insurance company sent me a brochure on grieving that listed the typical concerns of surviving widows and widowers. It listed financial security as the principal concern of widows, and household management as the widower's first concern. It did not at all describe my situation because I had made beds, vacuumed, shopped for food, and prepared meals during the frequent periods when she was disabled. I listed my needs at that time, and companionship was at the top of the list. We had made no promises regarding remarriage because I, at least, expected her to take whatever steps would make her happy without worrying about what I would have wanted. As for myself, I wasn't searching for anyone and had my work to keep me busy.

As I approach the end of my eighth decade, I realize more than ever that the great joys in life are more in the journey than in the destination. When faced with unfair or unforeseen obstacles, my motto is, "When fate gives you a lemon, make lemonade"; helpless wringing of hands is not my style, and I try to avoid blaming others for my failures and remain alert to opportunities. Much of a person's experience also depends on one's worldview: some see the world as a pie or a zero-sum game where a gain by one person must be at the expense of someone else; many of the world's troubles result from conduct based on that assumption. Others view life as a positive-sum game or a garden that can be cultivated to produce as much as necessary so that a person can gain without depriving someone else. I believe that I have profited from the efforts of people who cultivated the garden, and want to add my bit for the benefit of those who follow.

Measuring Turbulence

Completion of the Ph.D. in 1954 meant that a major decision had to be made concerning our future, and Wynonna and I carefully considered several alternatives. By that stage in my career, I had sufficient confidence in my success that I could take into account the way I might contribute to another goal: improving the general welfare of humankind. I was interviewed for jobs with Univac Computers in the Twin Cities, IBM in Endicott, New York, and Northwestern University in Evanston, Illinois. The offer from the Institute of Technology at Northwestern was so attractive that we were ready to accept if satisfactory housing could be found. When we looked for a home, the influence of "red-lining" was starkly demonstrated: the only homes the real estate agent would show us were badly run down and in unattractive neighborhoods. They cost less than we could have afforded, and we knew that the agent would not dare to show them to a white professor's family. Our final choice, the University of Iowa, was based on its favorable climate for the developing children, congenial colleagues, and an open community with many cosmopolitan features.

Iowa offered a tenure-track appointment as an assistant professor in the Department of Mechanics and Hydraulics, headed by Professor Howe, and a parallel appointment as research engineer at the Iowa Institute of Hydraulic Research, headed by Professor Rouse. The work was challenging, with access to excellent resources and world-class colleagues as well as professional travel to many parts of the world. I have enjoyed teaching every undergraduate course in the department at various times, as well as graduate courses in my specialties. My career developed rapidly, with promotion to associate professor with tenure in 1956 and to full professor in 1959. I credit Rouse and Howe with providing the opportunities and making the evaluations that promoted my professional development. They may not have been aware that I thereby became the first African American tenured professor in the history of the university, and would have considered it irrelevant. So do I. The large and highly productive teaching and research staff at the institute had long been and continues to be a microcosm of the world population, with women and men from every inhabited continent, including urban and rural America. I was simply a member of the human family, and only later did I learn that an irrational taboo had been dishonored by my appointment. Many years later, Howe commented to several people that my record was the strongest that he ever sent to the president with his recommendation for appointment.

My administrative experience leads me to view many events from the perspective of human rights, and to interpret the behavior of people in terms of humanitarian motives. As I review my relations with Dawson, Rouse, and Howe, described above, I see an interesting combination of their personal concern for an individual and impersonal dedication to standards of academic excellence. Dean Dawson helped many students with problems similar to mine, and his son John tells me that he financed several staff and student homes. His original support may have been inspired by an expectation that I would be a credit to the college, but it was an act of faith because I had not yet produced anything. Rouse and Howe also had a fatherly interest in my welfare, but were not particularly known as humanitarians. They supported me primarily on the basis of performance, and their work with students and fellow professionals in general demonstrated that sentiment did not take precedence before an adherence to academic standards.

My experience with Rouse illustrates our deepening friendship. Research at the institute required rather frequent travel, and I occasionally accompanied him to Washington, D.C. We could walk along for blocks without speaking; we felt at ease with one another. We especially liked seafood and often dined at the Captain's Table restaurant where we could get one of Rouse's favorite foods, cherrystone clams. He said that a small order of six was not enough, and that a full dozen were too many. We would therefore split a small and a large order so that each of us had nine. My experience was not unique — other colleagues have since related the same story of dining with him.

In retrospect, my procedure for career planning was rather unorthodox if not exceptional. I did not consult professional counselors or look at advertisements for positions, as my original decisions show: to attend college, select an academic major, pursue graduate study, and remain at the university after receiving the doctorate. My procedure has been to choose a particular option because it presents a challenge rather than a promise of guaranteed success, and then to deliver my best performance. I never had a long-range goal such as to be a titan of business, a bishop, an admiral, a dean, to win a Nobel Prize, or even to be a professor, but I believed that a job well done would lead to desirable options. In using that approach it is essential to remain sensitive to opportunities and evaluate them thoroughly so that one's career development is not in someone else's hands. Its main advantage is flexibility; one cannot see in advance many of the desirable options that result from a solid performance record. After a few years of administrative work, I was invited to speak as a guest to a class on career planning. After the professor heard my description of this unorthodox "planning," he quietly refrained from further invitations because it was not generally applicable.

Another advantage to my type of career development is that it permits consideration beyond a personal professional goal. As a family develops, the needs of a spouse and children should be taken into account; their welfare may suffer from a choice that is ideal for oneself. This is a particularly important example of a principle I utilized in discussions with students and underscored in the book *New Dawns*. My guiding star has been the welfare of humankind collectively *and individually*; actions in pursuit of a global goal or on behalf of people at a distance should not jeopardize the welfare of those close at hand.

My process of career development contrasts sharply with that of my mentor, Rouse. As related in a biographical sketch by two of his longtime colleagues, Professors John F. Kennedy and Enzo Macagno,

> Hunter was born in Toledo on 29 March, 1906, the only child of Henry Esmond Rouse, a hardware dealer, and Jesse Rouse, nee Hunter. He lost his father while still a child, and thereafter was reared by his mother and Adolph de Clair-mont, a French-born physician-scientist-inventor who was a close friend of the family and Hunter's godfather. De Clair-mont, a linguist and widely traveled man of broad interests, had a many faceted influence on him. . . . De Clairmont, Hunter's godfather, had implanted in him not only the aim of becoming a civil engineer but also that of studying in Europe (preferably at the Sorbonne), so the choice was an easy one. This was an important juncture in his career.

At that point in his life, at age twenty-three, Rouse knew that he wanted to be a hydraulic engineer, and he soon refined that goal by a decision to transform hydraulic engineering through application of the principles of classical mechanics. His life is an example of a brilliant man who dominated his environment, insisted on excellence in all that he undertook, and inspired everyone with whom he came in contact. He attracted students and staff from many countries, and so inspired them that students would remain after he had completed a lecture and copy his words and precise sketches from the blackboard. His national and international honors for teaching, research, and writing are proof that he was the recognized leader in his field.

Having "grown up" at the institute from my freshman year, I had learned much about the discipline of fluid mechanics and the techniques used in research, and when I began working full time I found that much of the work was handicapped by inadequate measuring instruments. My background in chemical and electrical engineering filled a gap in the skills of the research staff, and I gradually became the head of a special staff consisting primarily of undergraduate students in electrical engineering who worked part time to assist me with the development of electronic measuring instruments. My professional reputation was based on that specialty within the field, and most of my engineering publications were concerned with measurements in irrotational flow, turbulence, river hydraulics, and biomedical applications. The measurement and analysis of turbulence in water and air was the subject of my dissertation and most of my lecturing in the United States and abroad.

Lack of orthodoxy has marked much of my career development because I had no overall plan and responded to opportunities as they arose; the procedure I followed for my doctoral dissertation illustrates the process. Normally, a doctoral student and an advising professor agree on a topic and a plan of procedure, after which the student conducts the necessary research under the watchful eye of the adviser. That method worked well with most of the candidates in my department because they depended on the general research activities of the institute to provide ideas and support in the form of facilities and salaries. I relied on the ongoing institute research for ideas about needed instrumentation, but could not rely on the professors for guidance since I was filling the void in their skills. I established contact with researchers at laboratories such as Johns Hopkins University and at the National Bureau of Standards who were also developing instruments, and visited their laboratories for consultation when I needed reassurance. One might inquire, "How can the quality of the research be determined if the professors depend on the student to break new ground?" In my case, the answer was to publish the results of the research for evaluation by researchers all over the globe. My dissertation was so well accepted that it was reprinted as an institute paper that was still in demand long after I had moved on to administrative work.

Our research could be divided into two parts: that which solved immediate problems, and that which illuminated new principles without reference to a specific application. When the Iowa Highway Commission asked for help to prevent the collapse of county bridges during floods, the institute conducted studies in the laboratory that showed that bridges collapse because the supporting piers are undermined by the action of the fast-moving water at the height of the flood. This cause had not been suspected earlier because the sediment carried by the floodwaters filled in the hole as the waters receded. The conclusion needed verification, so we conducted tests on existing bridges in the field. No instruments were available for such studies, so I designed and built electric detectors and attached them to bridges on the Skunk River south of Ames and on the Centennial Bridge over the Mississippi River at Dubuque.

The U.S. Office of Naval Research provided a grant to support the development of my hot-wire and hot-film anemometers for measuring turbulence in water because of possible application in antisubmarine warfare. By detecting and following the underwater wake of a speeding submarine, it could be tracked down and destroyed if necessary. I also designed and built devices to detect very small pressure and velocity fluctuations in the water flowing through giant penstocks that conduct water to the turbines in the Fort Randall hydroelectric power plant on the Missouri River. The data thus collected helped the operators to reduce the erosion damage caused by cavitation near the walls of the penstocks. These examples show some of the ways that basic research, conducted for no specific purpose, can be applied to particular problems.

Those types of specialized research became the basis for my consulting and professional activities, and accounted for most of my national and international travel. Hubbard Instrument Company and Hubbard Consultants were created to serve the needs of researchers at other organizations that did not have the resources to replicate the devices I had placed in the public arena through publication in professional journals or internal laboratory reports. The instruments were constructed at the hydraulics laboratory with the assistance of John R. Glover, who began working for me while he was still an undergraduate in electrical engineering, and Ernest Schwab, a mechanic I trained as an electronics technician. I paid the institute a percentage of the receipts in exchange for the use of its facilities. Glover continued as head of the instrumentation laboratory after I left, and developed instruments for on-line analysis of flow data. Ernie later nominated me for university president when Sandy Boyd left for the Field Museum.

Research activities promoted my professional development and supplemented my modest salary during a period when the needs of our growing family were greatest. My university salary increased from $2,059 in 1946, the year that Philip was born, to $27,495 in 1972, the year that Peter graduated from high school. I did not fully develop the commercial enterprises because I preferred the academic life, and my reluctance to borrow money would have been a severe restriction to growth. Reflecting my deficiencies as a childhood salesman, my entrepreneurial instincts are quite weak; I have never been in danger of becoming wealthy.

Research was considered to be only half of my overall responsibilities, and each semester I regularly taught at least one undergraduate course in solid mechanics, fluid mechanics, or mechanics of materials. Additional sections of those courses were taught by teaching assistants under my supervision, so that twenty-five students were the normal class size. In addition, I taught graduate courses or seminars in fluid mechanics and electronic instrumentation, and was elected to the Graduate Council. After being appointed dean of academic affairs, I was surprised to find that the faculty in many departments considered nonsponsored research plus one course and a graduate seminar to be a normal load.

Research at the Iowa Institute of Hydraulic Research was rewarding to me because I could see that it was contributing to the solution of many problems of domestic and international importance. Controlling floods on rivers while improving agriculture through irrigation; preventing the destruction of bridges during floods; preventing erosion of beaches by the action of waves; development of hydroelectric power; and stabilizing the banks of rivers are examples of research directed to domestic problems. Research on those projects was sponsored by the Bureau of Public Roads, the Army Corps of Engineers (responsible for management of internal navigable waterways), the Bureau of the Interior, the Iowa State Highway Commission, the National Science Foundation, and private companies. The institution developed by Hunter Rouse and his pioneering predecessors has continued to advance under the direction of Professors John F. Kennedy and V. C. Patel, and I am pleased that a formal history has been published by the institute.

Reviewing my various activities, I am somewhat surprised to see how many of them relate to the military. Active army service is the most obvious, but much of my engineering research was sponsored by the Naval Research Laboratory, the Office of Naval Research, the Army Corps of Engineers, and the Rock Island Arsenal. From 1977 until 1983, I served on the board of visitors for Air University, the Air Force institution for continuing leadership education of its officers at all levels. I made many trips to Montgomery, Alabama, as a board member and came to know some generals who later served as advisers to presidents. I spoke at the Rock Island Arsenal on the subject "Making Sounder Choices," and to the ROTC at Coe College on the subject "Are Technologists Human?" For the university's ROTC commissioning ceremony in 1966, I gave the principal address on the subject "Educated Leadership — Fact or Dream?"

Most of my involvement with the military was by invitation rather than by design, and all of my research projects were morally "neutral" in themselves, applicable to either virtuous or evil uses: solving problems of turbulence is as important for the design of civilian airliners as of military craft, the principles of shock absorbers are as applicable to landing gear for airliners as for artillery guns, and developing the leadership skills of officers was entirely consistent with my university work. Except for my research during the war, I would not have been willing to conduct research that had no potential to benefit humankind aside from military applications.

My enlistment in the army and readiness to kill on command raise grave questions in my mind, however. I ask myself whether military service was consistent with a life dedicated to nonviolent resolution of conflict. To answer the question, I recall our mother's warning to my brothers and me: "If I find that you have started a fight, you will be punished. If I find that you did not fight back when attacked, you will be punished." Human history is an endless record of violent conflict, and aggressors are merciless if they prevail. Love is a virtue above all others, but it is difficult to love from the grave. I have great admiration for brave people who are conscientious objectors on principle, and could have made a case for myself if I had wished to do so. I did not so choose but joined the army willingly at a time when we had been mercilessly attacked, and I was willing to fire in anger if the need had arisen. There may be occasions, however, when I would demur on grounds of conscience if I believed that I would be serving an aggressor.

In 1951, I received a call from Margaret Petersen, a recent classmate who was then an engineer at Waterways Experiment Station in Vicksburg, Mississippi. She was arranging a program for an approaching annual meeting in Vicksburg of the hydraulics division of the American Society of Civil Engineers, and invited me to present a paper based on my research. I agreed to do so, and proceeded to prepare the paper. In a few weeks, she called again in great agitation to inform me that the managers of the hotel designated for the meeting would not permit my participation because of their strict segregation laws. The news came as a shock to Margaret, a gracious native of Iowa, and it was difficult for her to convey the news because of embarrassment about putting me in an awkward situation. She had been informed that if she insisted on having me speak, I would have to use the service elevator to reach the meeting room, deliver my speech, and immediately depart without further participation in the conference. That was unacceptable to either of us, of course, and a colleague from the institute, David Appel, presented my paper so that the session could proceed as planned. The hotel managers may have thought that they were teaching those Iowa Yankees a lesson about the realities of American life, but I saw the incident in the light of my childhood experience: the flaw was theirs, not ours. They were not only exposing the Achilles' heel of a regressive culture, but also retarding the development of their conference economy.

An interesting sequel to that occasion was an invitation in 1968, after I had become a full professor and dean, from the University of Mississippi School of Engineering to present the *first* (their emphasis) seminar in engineering science on the subject "Engineering Instrumentation." I accepted the invitation, was given red-carpet treatment with housing at the "Ole Miss" Alumni Center, and presented the paper to a large audience in Carrier Hall on the university campus. My hosts were very gracious, and I detected a look of pride on the face of the black waiter at the Alumni Center. In 1987, Petersen, by then a professor of engineering at the University of Arizona, was presented with an award as a distinguished alumna of the University of

Iowa on the basis of her outstanding record of teaching, research, and publication. I was honored to sit at her table for the recognition luncheon.

The years from 1946 until 1966 were a period of growth in my professional stature as well as the family, involving travel throughout the United States, Canada, Europe, South America, and Japan, meeting with professional colleagues and giving lectures. In my first trip abroad in 1956, I visited the hydraulics laboratory at Wallingford southwest of London and the charming laboratory of Sir Geoffrey Taylor at Emmanuel College of Cambridge University. Taylor's research was known for its acute insight, and his equipment was known for its simple elegance. I then traveled by train from London to Dover, across the English Channel on a ferry during the night, and through the Netherlands countryside to Paris. There I consulted with engineers at Electricité de France and was wined and dined at a four-star restaurant by the commandant, a staff member whose principal responsibility was to entertain official visitors to the laboratory. Finally, I consulted with engineers and scientists at the National Hydraulics Laboratory in Zurich, Switzerland. On a later visit to the Neyrpic Laboratory in Grenoble, I gave lectures on the hot-wire anemometer (the subject of my Ph.D. dissertation) and took a side trip to Chamonix and Mont Blanc in the French Alps. There was also adequate time on the trip to see a play at the Garrick Theater in London and a performance of *La Plume de ma tante* in Paris, as well as to visit some of the usual tourist attractions — the Eiffel Tower and the Cathedral of Notre Dame, for example. In each of my several trips to Paris, I spent as much time as possible in the magnificent Louvre.

In summer 1962, I spent four weeks at University of the Republic in Buenos Aires, Argentina, lecturing and guiding research as a consultant for the Organization of American States (OAS). To prepare for the trip, I studied Spanish at the high school and the university. With the indispensable help of Macagno at the institute (a native of Argentina), we translated some of my key documents into Spanish for distribution to students and colleagues in Buenos Aires and Montevideo, Uruguay. I was able to read my lectures in miserably poor Spanish, but needed help in understanding questions from the class.

The College of Engineering was in a beautiful building that had been constructed by Juan Perón in honor of his beloved wife Eva. It was finished in imported Italian marble with a different color for each floor, but was in a state of disarray because Perón was in exile in Spain. The city was in constant turmoil, and entering the building meant running a gauntlet of political demonstrators. Only one entrance was open to discourage theft of the furnishings, but it was a futile effort; even the toilet seats were missing. Representatives of the OAS had warned me to move about with caution and avoid crowds, so I started to take a detour when I saw a large crowd ahead on the Avenida Florida. On closer observation, I saw that the crowd was strangely quiet and orderly, so I continued. Upon arrival, I heard the reason for the gathering and the quiet attention. Loudspeakers had been placed on the sidewalk in front of a music shop, and the beautiful contralto voice of Marian Anderson filled the air, singing "He's Got the Whole World in His Hands." I knew that a crowd listening in rapt attention to a spiritual in a foreign language represented no danger, and I joined them. I gave lectures in other universities as part of my official duties, and two Mormon missionaries approached me when I lectured in Córdoba. They had read about my visit in the local newspaper, and came to meet a fellow American in that out-of-the-way location.

In spring 1965, I joined nine other engineers and scientists for a two-week tour of major research institutions in Japan under the sponsorship of the National Science Foundation and the Japan Science Society. It was a splendid cultural and professional experience. We ate many special meals with Japanese counterparts (with geisha girls as hostesses), rode the famous high-speed train, and went to an outstanding theater performance in Osaka preceded by a formal tea. After the official travel had ended, I flew to Sapporo for a visit with a former colleague at Iowa, Dr. Mikio Arie, who was later selected as president of the University of Hokkaido. He arranged for me to stay at a delightful inn overlooking the Sea of Japan where no one spoke English, beds (thick mattresses on the floor) were assembled when needed, and group baths included both genders. After I had registered, he served as interpreter to inform the staff what time I wished to retire and what I wanted for breakfast. I had the honor of visiting his family in their home, a rare treat because the Japanese custom is to entertain guests in restaurants or other public places. In 1993, Arie was selected by the University of Iowa Alumni Association to receive the Distinguished Alumni Award.

Later in 1965, I received a Fulbright-Hays grant for travel to Chile as a research scholar. I had planned to take the entire family, but we canceled our plans because I had just accepted an appointment as dean and needed to get started.

In 1968, I was selected again for a Fulbright-Hays scholarship to lecture at universities in Caracas, Rio de Janeiro, São Paolo, and Buenos Aires on the way to Montevideo, where I spent four weeks in cooperative research with engineering faculty at National University of the Republic of Uruguay. The lectures were repeated at the national universities in Santiago, Chile; Lima, Peru; and Quito, Ecuador, on the way home. It was an especially noteworthy trip because I was accompanied by Wynonna, Phil, Rick, and Peter, who explored on their own when I was busy with professional activities. My schedule allowed time for me to travel with the family because it included an unusually large number (by American standards) of holidays.

From 1972 to 1977, I served as a consultant to the U.S. Agency for International Development, and learned as much about other cultures as I contributed to the solution of their problems. International applications were especially important to me because many of them related to assisting people in less-developed countries, such as controlling the floods that ravaged them annually, using stored water to irrigate crops, developing hydroelectric power in places that had no coal or oil, and improving engineering education. Working with these countries taught me the importance of understanding the culture of the people we were trying to assist. To convince farmers to adopt improved techniques, it was necessary to consult not only with the national agricultural official, but also with the most respected farmer in the village. When washers and dryers were placed in remote villages to relieve the drudgery of washing laundry in a stream, we found that the women preferred the stream because washing was more than a chore — it was a social occasion. Farmers readily adopted tractors in place of human or animal labor, but minor breakdowns caused tractors to stand idle in the field; farmers lacked the experience of maintaining mechanical equipment, which we had taken for granted.

When economic development required large-scale cultivation of cash crops, we had to plan land use so that each farmer could have a traditional family plot near the neighbors. This was achieved by placing several family garden units in a central cluster, with large fields for the cash crop radiating outward. Construction of major projects, such as a dam that would inundate a large area, required special consideration because of the disruption of lifestyles and relocation involved. Although we were experts on technical feasibility, serious mistakes could be made by underrating the environmental impact on the people. Perhaps most important, we learned to consult with intended beneficiaries to learn of *their* priorities, rather than assuming that we could determine the greatest need from a distance.

In my travels abroad, especially in trips off the usual tourist routes, I saw firsthand the contrast between affluent neighborhoods and the favelas of Brazil, the shantytowns in South Africa, and the villages of India, for example. I have long been concerned about hunger and homelessness in the United States, and have devoted much of my career to offering opportunity to people caught in a vicious poverty cycle through no fault of their own. However, seeing firsthand the hopeless poverty of the Third World illuminated a new dimension. The great chasm between rich and poor in America is inexcusable in a land of affluence, but the poor of the Third World have even worse prospects of escaping their plight. I have contributed to a solution to the problem through my work with the U.S. Agency for International Development, but I have modified my criticism of American businesses that pay substandard wages in their foreign operations. My goal has always been to bridge the gulf between economically advanced nations and those lesser developed, but I realize that the goal cannot be accomplished in a single stroke. Even substandard wages are better than other available options; they inject hard money into societies with desperate need and can be likened to girders in bridges over the gulf of international prosperity/poverty. Moreover, earned wages are superior to income that might trickle down from international block grants to governments, because the workers are exercising skills needed to elevate their national economies. The direct employment of people also represents a better use of America's wealth than the provision of weapons, too often used by local governments to deny the legitimate aspirations of the oppressed citizens. As the pressure of competition improves their bargaining position, Third World workers will have a greater ability to demand their share. The permanence of the benefit will depend on whether citizens can protect their interests through democratic governments.

In my international contacts, I learned much about the means people use to cope with weak economies in urban areas. When Professor Jose Gandolfo, my host at the University of Argentina, parked his car, he reminded me that I had left my hat on the seat. I told him that it was an old hat that I used only when it was raining, and he said, "I'm not concerned about your hat: it's my window they will break to reach your old hat." Before leaving, he removed the windshield wiper blades and hid them inside the car. He explained that wiper blades were a common target of thieves. When I wondered whether there was a market for used blades, he responded, "Certainly there is; the thieves create the demand when they steal blades." In Montevideo, men wearing aprons walked for several blocks carrying a small tray waiter-style with a single bottle of a soft drink. When my host professor in Quito parked his car, two little boys offered to guard it while we were gone. The professor paid them without hesitation, and responded to my question about the need for protection. "I'm not buying protection; it's extortion, because those boys are the ones who would vandalize the car if I didn't pay." In Kathmandu, a charming little girl about ten years old, speaking excellent English, sold prayer wheels in the outdoor market. She insisted that I buy one, and I was so impressed by her persistence and obvious intelligence that I paid her and said she could keep the wheel. Later, the hotel clerk explained that she was not as alone as it appeared; some adult, possibly her father, was probably watching from a nearby bench and would pocket the money as soon as I was out of sight. A bright child could sell many more prayer wheels than an adult could. I wished I could have adopted the child and enrolled her in an American school.

None of my domestic or international travel expenses were

supported by university funds. Business travel expenses were paid from grants and contracts until I entered the administration and no longer had external support.

I served on many boards and committees that gave me an opportunity to learn about organizations outside academia, including membership and then as chairman of the board of visitors for General Motors Institute (GMI), a technical college owned by General Motors. It is located in Flint, Michigan, and offers degrees in business administration and automotive engineering. GMI was treated as a division of the corporation, so when the oil crisis of 1974 led to a general 33 percent reduction in head count (total number of regular employees), the reduction applied to GMI as well as the production divisions. To soften the impact on the educational programs, GMI contracted out some functions such as custodial and dining services, but the goal could not be met without reducing the number of faculty. The results were little short of catastrophic, because professors who thought they had permanent tenure were forced to retire early or simply leave with severance pay. Stress-related ailments such as strokes, heart disease, and hypertension increased substantially, alerting me to possible effects of a financial emergency at the university.

After the crisis was over, committee members were offered the opportunity to participate in the Assigned Car Program for unclassified (that is, upper-level) executive personnel. Each of us was assigned a new GM vehicle every three months. No restriction was placed on the distance the cars could be driven; the only restrictions were that we had to rotate our choices through each of the five divisions — Chevrolet, Pontiac, Buick, Oldsmobile, and Cadillac — but no limousines or the Chevrolet Corvette. That was quite an experience for someone who had always treated cars as little more than basic transportation.

From 1971 to 1973, I was a consultant to the National Institutes of Health as a member of the visiting committee for the National Institute for General Medical Sciences. That was an interesting assignment that required me to serve on evaluation committees for some of the top hospitals in the country and review proposals for research support from NIH.

In 1970, I served on a panel of the Academy for Educational Development to conduct a role and scope study of Tuskegee

Institute. The panel included Andrew Brimmer, Federal Reserve commissioner, and the panel visited Tuskegee several times before presenting its final report in New York City. My family accompanied me on that occasion, and we spent two days in the presidential suite at the New York Hilton because the hotel had overbooked and could not honor our reservation owing to the extended visit of a Middle East head of state.

For many years, I was the alternate to the president as the university representative on the Iowa Coordinating Council for Postsecondary Education. The experience gave me insight into interactions among public and independent colleges, and increased my high regard for the area college system and its role in preparing students for emerging employment demands.

Although we were quite happy with life at the university and I never applied for any openings elsewhere, I was nominated or invited to apply for some very attractive positions at other institutions. In all cases, I steadfastly refused to use outside offers as bargaining chips; an offer was either accepted or rejected without asking the University of Iowa for any concession. One early offer was especially interesting: perhaps one year after obtaining my bachelor's degree, I was visited by Des Moines attorney S. Joe Brown, my Sunday school teacher during the high school years. He had received degrees from the University of Iowa in philosophy (1898) and law (1901) and taught briefly at Bishop College, a small liberal arts institution in Marshall, Texas. He offered me a position on the faculty at Bishop, but I replied that a bachelor's degree in engineering and no teaching experience did not seem to qualify me to teach at a liberal arts college. His response was my first glimmer of understanding the quality of education in the former slave states: "You could teach any of the courses they offer, and I am sure that they would welcome someone with a degree from a northern university." My understanding increased greatly when, nearly twenty years later, William McMillan, president of Rust College in Mississippi, visited the Iowa campus as part of a cooperative arrangement between the two institutions. He explained their challenge: take incoming high school graduates with the equivalent of an eighth-grade education, and bring them up to the bachelor level in four years. I now realize that I indeed could have made a significant contribution by teaching at Bishop College, but hope that I have made an even greater contribution to the education of African Americans by working with others to bring the resources of a great university to assist historically black colleges and universities.

When Boyd resigned as president in 1981 to assume a similar position at the Field Museum in Chicago, I saw an opportunity to resume my tenured position as professor of engineering and to give an incoming president the freedom to select his or her own core administrators. Complete preparations were made for the move: money was allocated to the College of Engineering for my salary and supporting expenses, and I received a developmental assignment for one year so that I could prepare for the specialty of water power engineering, which the Department of Mechanical Engineering had designated as a priority need. With support from the National Science Foundation and possibly from the Department of Energy and other foundations, I arranged appointments as a visiting professor in electrical engineering at the University of California in Berkeley and visiting engineer with an engineering friend at Bechtel, Inc. in San Francisco, a global leader in the design and production of equipment to generate electric power.

My plans were changed before reaching a final stage when newly appointed president James O. Freedman asked me to postpone my leave until he arrived. I complied with his request, and continued with my responsibilities for the student services and Center for the Arts through his tenure as president as well as that of Hunter Rawlings III. With Freedman's support, I developed programs for outstanding undergraduate scholars, and developed the Opportunity at Iowa program under Rawlings. I now believe that I made a greater contribution to the university through that period than I would have made as a retread professor in a new specialty at age sixty. Perhaps I was diverted from the highest calling of a scholar, but not from a chance to continue with what had become an important part of my mission — to provide exceptional students with the best education we can offer, and to extend to minority and low-income students the opportunities I have enjoyed.

7

Filling a Void

Although my hopes for a professional career and a family were being fulfilled while the children were growing, something was missing. To fill my personal void I supplemented family and engineering faculty activities by becoming involved with many colleagues in community programs directed to children and to people in need, such as Boy Scouts and working to improve the conditions for the less fortunate citizens in Iowa City. While I was president of the Iowa City Kiwanis club we established a sheltered workshop that eventually evolved into Goodwill Industries of Southeast Iowa. I also served on the board of directors of the Iowa City Consumers Cooperative Society that provided area farmers with tires, batteries, fence posts, wire, and fuel. We later opened a downtown market to sell groceries. The co-op experience was especially enjoyable because I became well acquainted with the farmers and their families, visiting in their homes and speaking in their churches. Their independent attitude and acceptance of new acquaintances on the basis of individual qualities contrasted with an often-repeated stereotype of clannishness and rigidity. When people I met in my far-flung travels asked about Iowa's character as an agricultural state, I was pleased to assure them I had many warm friends who were farmers, and they were expert business managers and actively involved in the larger world.

I taught in and served as general superintendent of the Sunday school in the First United Methodist Church, served on the official board of the church, delivered baccalaureate sermons, and served on the board of the Wesley Foundation. Some of my happiest duties were handing out their own Bibles to third-graders, and assisting other volunteers in transporting severely disabled children to Sunday school from the hospital school operated by the university hospital. A program sponsored by the Rock Island Arsenal enabled superior high school students to spend a summer at the university working as interns to faculty conducting research. When one of my interns was a Methodist, I took him to church, to the delight of his parents in Oregon.

I spoke on subjects related to human rights in Methodist churches in rural Johnson County, Bettendorf, Marshalltown, and Williamsburg. I gave commencement addresses at several colleges, and an address in 1966 to help celebrate the ninety-ninth anniversary of Johnson C. Smith University in North Carolina, and at Jackson State College in Mississippi. Later, I was awarded the Doctor of Humanities degree from St. Ambrose University after delivering their commencement address, and served eighteen years on its board of directors. In 1985, Wynonna accompanied me to Lamoni, Iowa, when I gave the commencement address at Graceland College, an institution operated by the Reorganized Church of Jesus Christ, Latter Day Saints.

I seldom mentioned religion to students unless they chose to attend meetings of religious organizations in which I was involved. We were quite conscious of the First Amendment restriction regarding church and state, and I was careful to maintain a neutral stance. That did not mean that religious activities were restricted, and student organizations of many denominations used university facilities for their programs, including worship services. I felt an obligation to accommodate students who wanted and needed religious guidance, and my principal method of assistance was to cooperate with campus ministers who were assigned by several denominations to serve students on campus. The activities were personally rewarding, but had small influence in the larger world and over the long range.

When Prince Edward County in Virginia closed its public schools in 1960 rather than obey the court order to integrate them, private schools were established to accommodate white children, but none were provided for African Americans. The American Friends Service Committee quickly started an emergency program to relocate the neglected children to families in host communities outside of Virginia, and several families formed a group named Iowa City Sponsors for Equal Education. Three of the families accepted a visiting student in their home, provided room and board, and enrolled them in the Iowa City schools as a member of the family. Transportation to Iowa and health insurance were paid by the American Friends Service Committee, and funds were raised locally for tuition, personal expenses, books and supplies, and emergency clothing needs for the Iowa winters.

All three students were from Farmville, Virginia: James Lee lived with a professor in the school of religion, Robert Michaelson, and his wife Florence; Otis Wiley lived with a professor in the Department of Internal Medicine, William Connor, and his wife Selma; and our guest was James Brown, who was two years older than Phil. Our children made friends with James, and it was a healthy experience for everyone. Later, we provided a similar home for Luvert Walker of Mississippi, who went on to college and now teaches in Pittsfield, New York. Dr. and Mrs. Connor hosted another student from Virginia, James Ghee, who graduated from high school, enrolled in the University of Iowa, graduated with honors, and then became one of the first African Americans to graduate from the University of Virginia Law School.

I had never been involved in politics directly but gave my support to action-oriented organizations such as the NAACP, which Wynonna and I joined as life members in 1957. I also contributed to individual campaigns, and usually voted for people in both major parties, to force me to think carefully about the issues. It was sometimes difficult to find an acceptable Republican, but I regularly voted for Eisenhower, Robert Ray, and, until 1994, James Leach. Ike's warning about the "military/industrial complex" impressed me as highly appropriate, and has been confirmed by our cold war experience, during which vast sums of money flowed into the pockets of the already wealthy through the pipeline of "national defense." Ray's moderate and sensible policies and priorities led me to say that I would vote for him regardless of the office he sought. I admire Leach's pursuit of campaign finance reform and his courageous vote for the discharge petition to bring it to floor against the wishes of his hard-liner colleagues. I will support politicians of any party whose votes are guided by a concern for the welfare of average and less fortunate Americans, as opposed to an incessant harping for tax relief on behalf of the wealthy. I prefer to ask, "How can we improve our educational system, assure health care for all, provide a safety net for the less fortunate and those with disabilities, and preserve the natural heritage of the country?" In contrast, others ask, "How can I increase my personal wealth without limit, and the devil take the hindmost?" They fail to recognize that, like it or not, we share a common destiny and that a rapidly increasing discrepancy in wealth is incompatible with a stable democracy.

The intense activities associated with civil rights during the 1960s spurred me to write to Iowa senators Jack Miller and Bourke Hickenlooper asking them to support the Civil Rights Act of 1965. Republican Hickenlooper responded that

> Such things as the equality of voting rights and opportunities, non-discrimination between individuals solely on the grounds of race, etc., should be safeguarded. . . . However, there are several provisions in the [Civil Rights] bill that may create additional Federal powers which, in effect, could be abused by emotionally or politically oriented administrators to the point where the discretion and responsibility of individuals for their own affairs could be seriously eroded.

I had been alerted to possible problems with the senator when, in a speech in Cedar Rapids, Roy Wilkins of the NAACP criticized his voting record on civil rights. J. B. Morris, longtime publisher of the *Iowa Bystander*, Iowa's leading newspaper for African Americans, was a rock-ribbed Republican who remained loyal to the Great Emancipator long after his party had eloped with the Dixiecrats, and he wrote an editorial defending Hickenlooper. Hickenlooper was grateful for Morris's support and purchased a large ad in the *Bystander* announcing his vote to confirm Thurgood Marshall for the Supreme Court. True to form, Hickenlooper voted with the opponents of the Civil Rights Act on the weakening amendments, then voted "yes" on the final bill.

Republican Miller responded that he had been carefully studying the bill, and proposed some amendments to improve it. He eventually voted for the bill and I was encouraged by the outcome, although I do not believe my inquiry was a factor.

A local issue soon stimulated my interest in politics. Although I did not realize it at the time, my support for an Iowa City ordinance in summer 1964 propelled me into the public spotlight and led indirectly to a radical change in my career. Until then, I had concentrated on professional and family activities, using social action and church work to meet my desire to help others rather than becoming actively involved in politics. I am not inclined toward introspection, and only recognized the impact of my new involvement years later when Rawlings asked why I was usually addressed as "Mr. Hubbard." I also was puzzled by the practice because it was not universal — I never minded when an occasional student would call me "Phil," as did some of the people on my staff, and of course, my many friends. The practice may have started when Boyd came into the administration, because he followed the law school custom in which students and faculty addressed one another as "Mr." or "Ms." When I read some of my almost-forgotten files to prepare them for the university archives, I realized how much of my philosophy and personality were revealed in some widely publicized speeches and interviews on political subjects and student protest activities. People had begun to view me in a new light, and I see no better way to explain the process than to use contemporary documents.

Events of the past may sometimes be perceived through rose-colored glasses or selective memories. To minimize that tendency, I present excerpts from my speech to the Iowa City Kiwanis club regarding a proposed ordinance on fair housing. The speech was inspired by a statement by Rev. L. D. Soens, principal of Regina High School and chairman of the Iowa City Human Relations Commission: "Indifference may damage the cause of the proposed housing ordinance more than any other single factor." I concluded that something should be done, and chose a speaking campaign as the way I could act as an individual not representing any organization. My first speech to the Iowa City Kiwanis Club on August 3, 1964, sheds light on some of my experience and basic philosophies and may also illustrate the problem-solving approach of an engineer.

When I agreed to speak on the subject of fair or open housing in Iowa City a week ago, . . . no opposition had been expressed, and it seemed reasonable to assume that the proposed ordinance would be passed and would receive the general support of the community. . . .

Since then, however, open opposition has been expressed by the Iowa City Board of Realtors, followed by the Iowa City Builders Association. . . .

Now I know, of course, that some of you belong to these organizations, and you may be uneasy about my speaking on this subject at this time. Well, you can relax. I have no intention of accepting you as adversaries. We have been friends for many years; I have taught your sons in the University [at that time, there were few if any women in the College of Engineering, and none in my classes], and your children in Sunday School. I have worked with your wives in my capacity as superintendent of the Sunday School, in the Iowa City Council–Manager Association, and in other civic and professional groups. You have accepted me as a member of Kiwanis and as a neighbor. I am proceeding on the assumption that you are fair and decent citizens who want to do what is right, and that you are unsure about how a change might affect your personal welfare. . . .

I will not reject you at this time any more than I would reject a brother who came down with the smallpox. . . . No, I do not see you as antagonists but rather as potential allies whose cooperation is essential if the problem of unfair discrimination is to be solved. In effect, I am here to enlist your help together with that of every citizen of Iowa City and the surrounding community in realizing the aims of a democratic society: To achieve justice for *all*.

. . . Last year, our City Council appointed a Commission on Human Relations to study the problems which exist in the community as a result of unfair discrimination, to recommend remedial action, and to educate the citizenry.

Surveys were conducted by this Commission and by the League of Women Voters. These surveys indicate that there is a great deal of discrimination in housing in Iowa City and that housing is the most pressing problem facing non-whites in our community. . . .

I can assure you that a survey was not necessary for me. I have rented rooms in three homes in Iowa City; I have rented one apartment for my family; I have bought two houses. In every case, the task was approached with uncertainty and apprehension because of the apparently universal unwillingness of owners and landlords to rent to members of minority groups, particularly Negroes. . . . In one case, an owner asked that a neighborhood survey be conducted before he answered my offer to buy (at a price in excess of the one he eventually accepted). The result? He decided against selling the property at that time. Since he was a decent man (head of a department at SUI) he did in fact rent out the house for one year before finally selling it.

The proposed ordinance would have protected me from the humiliation of a rejection by people whose fears later proved to be without foundation. (I now live in the same general area and no catastrophes have occurred.) Equally important, the owner would not have been put to the embarrassment and chagrin he must have suffered in resorting to such a transparent tactic as well as the financial loss he suffered in the transaction.

It has become a common experience to see elected representatives return from Des Moines or Washington and boast to their constituents of all the proposals they have blocked, and this in the name of conservatism! I submit that this is a cruel parody of the true spirit of conservatism. It belongs in the world of Alice in Wonderland or wrong-way Corrigan, who left New York for California and ended up in Paris. A true conservative, it seems to me, would do precisely the opposite. Go to Des Moines or Washington and tell fellow legislators, "We had that problem in my district and this is how we solved it. I suggest that you benefit from our experience, adapt our solution to your conditions, and secure justice. If you will not or cannot do this, a solution will have to be imposed because injustice cannot be permitted to continue indefinitely." Such an approach would have the effect of uniting groups within a community and would be truly progressive. Such a man would not be the object of the derision and scorn which so angers certain legislators today.

One might consider how this ideal procedure could be related to organizations other than government — for example, a state or national realtor's association. Should such an organization be an agency through which edicts from Big Brother are passed out to the faithful, to be applied blindly without regard to local conditions? Should the conditions in New York, Atlanta or Los Angeles, analyses which confuse cause with effect, or information based on myths be used to determine what should be done in Iowa City? I submit to you that this process is also topsy-turvy. Local citizens who operate under the protection of a public license should seek information for their guidance from the best available local source, calling upon generally respected experts, professionals, and other citizens who have both a broad experience and a local acquaintance. They should apply their professional judgment to this information in conducting their operations.

When they go to the state or national meeting they should pass on the knowledge they have gained and explain how they solved problems in their own community. This is again a positive approach to a complicated set of conditions, and allows adequate room for each individual to operate within the bounds of his or her own conscience. Each of us is a citizen of our community as well as a practitioner of an occupation, and our daily life must take into account both of these roles. This procedure need not be bad business, and it is a serious mistake to assume that moral behavior is incompatible with turning a profit. Whatever is best for the community will be most profitable in the long run. It is intended to protect the conscientious builder or realtor from unreasonable pressure from a third party as much as it protects the buyer. In the end analysis, it will protect the prejudiced person or the bigot from himself, because I believe that one cannot achieve his full stature as a person without self-respect. It is becoming increasingly difficult for anyone who professes to a religious belief to support racism in its various forms or to deny everyday courtesies to those of different religious belief.

Let us return to Iowa City and the ordinance. Ordinances should not be enacted for the benefit of 1%, 51%, or 90% of the population. *Everyone* should benefit, and I believe that this ordinance meets that criterion. I do not believe it was the intent of the Human Rights Commission or of the City Council that this ordinance should stand between buyer and seller, agent and client, landlord and tenant, lender and borrower, Catholic or Jew and Protestant. It is the intent of the sponsors that this ordinance should stand between all of these people on the one hand versus the forces of misinformation, intolerance and bigotry on the other hand. . . .

Now, what do I propose that we who are in this room should do? Get behind this ordinance; tell your mayor and the other councilmen that you will support them in restoring the deleted parts and in strengthening it. Assure them that you will support it after it is passed, and then proceed to do just that. . . .

This is your golden opportunity to make a vital contribution toward solving a critical national problem by your example. In one stroke, you can apply those ideals which seem so elusive in practical matters to improve your community *and* your business. Builders make a profit by selling houses, not by withholding them; realtors make commissions by promoting sales, not by discouraging them; lenders collect interest through well-secured loans, not by using their positions to pay homage to social myths. This ordinance will remove a millstone from your necks if you will use it properly. As a bonus, you will be able to face your clergyman on Sunday.

Practically, how can we make this ordinance work as it should? The first step is to obtain sound, reliable information, and I don't mean from Big Brother; not from New York, Atlanta or Los Angeles; not from a bunch of do-gooders in some other locality. Don't peddle biological, social or economic myths. We have an exceptional community here, with experts in every field which touches on this matter. Call on them for information; ask them to speak to your local societies so that you can discuss your particular problem. Our own Clyde Kohn is a nationally recognized authority in urban geography. Lyle Shannon and his department of Sociology and Anthropology can be a valuable source of reliable information. Arthur Bonfield in the College of Law has just completed an intensive study of state civil rights laws and their effects; we have specialists in economics, political science and history who will gladly contribute their services for this cause.

If you think that these are ivory tower dwellers unfamiliar with the realities of real life, just remember that they live in houses of brick and mortar, wood and concrete. Their equity in their homes represents a large part of their net worth, and they are just as interested in protecting it as you are interested in turning a profit. Then ask the personnel managers of our University, the veterans hospital, and our other industries what effect such an ordinance might have on their ability to secure the best staff available. The University Committee on Human Rights will help in any way that it can. To the extent that I am able, I offer my services as liaison with any person or group that you wish to consult.

Finally, after we have made Iowa City a better place to live, tell other communities how we did it. If we can't do it, then who in the world can? Where will you find a better community for the intelligent citizenry which is essential for Plato's dream of democracy in action?

No, my friends, I am not accepting any of you as adversaries. I'm asking for much more. Iowa City needs your help. The time is now. The problem is here. The solution is within our grasp. Let's make democracy work.

In its issue of August 7, 1964, the *Daily Iowan* reported on my speech to the Iowa City Rotary Club the previous day.

A plea to the Iowa City Board of Realtors and the Home Builders Association to reconsider their stand in opposition to the proposed fair housing ordinance was made Thursday by Philip Hubbard, SUI professor of mechanics and hydraulics.

"I humbly ask, not that you simply withdraw your opposition to the ordinance, but that you give a resounding 'aye' during your turn at the podium. Not for me, not for downtrodden minority groups, but for yourselves and every other citizen of Iowa City," Hubbard said. . . .

"When I have read of the opposition and apparent insensitivity to moral values on the part of realtors in Des Moines or some other city, I have conjured up visions of Shylock conspiring with Simon Legree. When the opponents of our own ordinance are men I have known and respected for many years, however, the picture changes radically.

"Therefore it is with a sense of foreboding that I find myself in apparent opposition with these men, and I realize that our confusion in Iowa City is part of a larger melange in our state and our nation; a situation in which friend suddenly seems to be foe, in which virtue seems to be vice, in which darkness illuminates the scene. . . .

"And when a visitor from the South tells me or when I read in a letter to the editor that 'the Negroes in the North are not like those in the South,' I pause and I ponder. And I have to admit that they are right. I'm not like the Negroes in Mississippi and Alabama.

"I only had one and a half strikes against me when I was born. True, I was born black, but my parents had not been driven to the depths of frustration and despair, and I grew up in a half-open community."

I made similar speeches to the Optimists and other clubs in Iowa City; all were covered in depth by the regional media, and the speeches were used as evidence of concrete examples of discrimination by supporters of the ordinance.

Since I was not a threat to anyone and had no official standing in the community, my appeal would have had little practical effect without the endorsement of community leaders, especially those who had the respect of the real estate lobby. To their great credit, the CEOs of the city's financial and industrial institutions came forth and gave their public support: Clark Houghton, president of the First National Bank; Jack Newman, general manager of the local Procter and Gamble plant; Charles

Dore, president of Owens Brush Company; and Arne Arneson, general manager of the J. C. Penney store, for example. Their support reassured the general community, the city council took a stand, and the ordinance was duly approved and became a model for such legislation. Having been initiated into direct citizen advocacy, I followed my own advice to the real estate representatives and wrote a letter to the editor in support of civil rights legislation at the state level, which was published in the *Des Moines Register* on November 4, 1964.

Community activities not only filled my personal void, but led indirectly and inadvertently to a change of career that I will discuss in later chapters.

III

The Administrative Years

A Career Branch

Even though I did not suspect it at the time, my community activities and speeches during the discussion of a fair housing ordinance in 1964 led to the end of my halcyon days of teaching and research in engineering. Transition to an administrative position began in 1963 with a phone call from President Virgil M. Hancher, asking me to serve as one of three faculty representatives on the newly created Committee on Human Rights. Another faculty member was my friend and "birthday twin," political science professor Donald B. Johnson (we were born on the same day, he in Minnesota, I in Missouri). Others on the original committee were students Edward Bennett of Newton and Elizabeth Brogan of Thornton and alumni William G. Nusser Sr. and Samuel Saltzman, both from Iowa City. Professor Boyd of the College of Law, one of the university's most affirmative and effective promoters of human rights, was appointed as chair. The committee's charge was based on the newly revised Human Rights Policy, which stated in part:

> The State University of Iowa brings together in common pursuit of its educational goals persons of many nations, races and creeds. The University is guided by the precept that

in no aspect of its programs shall there be differences in the treatment of persons because of race, creed, color or national origin and that equal opportunity and access to facilities shall be available to all. This principle is expected to be observed in the admission, housing, and education of students; in policies governing programs of extracurricular life and activities; and in the employment of faculty and staff personnel. The University shall work cooperatively with the community in furthering this principle.

The assignment fit very well into my civil rights activities, and I anticipated with pleasure working with students, university employees, business and religious leaders, and general community representatives cooperating to change a paternalistic system that treated some members of the university community as second-class citizens. Furthermore, in our own small way, we might make a difference at the national level by sharing our efforts with the other institutions with which we interacted.

When Howard Bowen succeeded Virgil Hancher as president in 1964, he appointed Boyd as vice president for academic affairs, and the two of them moved the university ahead in giant strides to support human rights within the larger world as well as in the university. In 1965, a crisis in the College of Engineering led to the appointment of Boyd as acting dean of engineering, and he asked me to assist him in restoring the faculty's badly eroded morale. I had a good background for the task, knew all of the engineering faculty personally and interviewed each one individually to obtain their opinions, and prepared a summary for Boyd. The experience taught me a valuable lesson about conflict resolution, and Boyd and I increased our knowledge of each other. The crisis ceased when Rouse reluctantly accepted the position of dean in spite of his long-stated conviction that teaching and research were the highest calling. As dean, he was responsible for appointing his successor as director of IIHR, and he lived up to his reputation for excellent judgment by bringing John F. Kennedy from MIT to fill the vacancy.

The scholarly Bowen often went to a summer retreat to think, and when he returned in fall 1965 he had produced a document creating a new position, associate dean of faculties, reporting to the vice president for academic affairs. A search committee including Professors Richard Lloyd-Jones and Allan Vestal was appointed, and they recommended me for the job. I considered the resulting offer, and after looking at my credentials, Bowen and Boyd decided to change the title to dean of academic affairs in recognition of my senior status in the faculty. I saw an opportunity to achieve my nontechnical goals in a larger arena and accepted it, even though it would interrupt and possibly terminate my successful career in engineering. I explored this topic in a paper I prepared for a College of Engineering symposium on "Technology and the Spirit of Man" in summer 1968. I was also reluctant to change careers because I believe, as many professors do, that the highest calling is in teaching and related scholarly activities, and do not regard an administrative appointment as an academic promotion. Since administrators have a decisive influence on academic freedom and the resources that are available for scholarly work, professors cannot place their welfare in the hands of managers whose priorities may not be in harmony with theirs, and should accept administrative duties for at least a limited number of years. I accepted the offer with some sadness; my mentor, Rouse, felt that I was making a mistake and I did not want to disappoint him.

As soon as I was named to the position, Boyd wanted me to move to Old Capitol, even though it was September and my new appointment would not be official until January 1. I had already agreed to teach two courses and was grappling with a vexing problem in the hot-wire anemometer. He was insistent, so I moved to my new office in the northeast corner of Old Capitol that was completely furnished and staffed with a personal secretary, Dianne Bodeen. Most of the books needed for my research were left in the old office in the hydraulics laboratory, and I moved back and forth on my bicycle between the two locations and my classes in the engineering building. The vexing research problem was solved by Jack Glover, who assumed responsibility for the instrumentation research.

My first assignment in the new position was to provide administrative assistance to faculty and students who were assisting two black colleges in Mississippi and Tennessee in support of the civil rights movement. Many people in Johnson County were among the leaders to promote the nationwide concern for liberation, and Iowa City had been among the first communities to adopt fair housing ordinances. One group formed the Mississippi Support program (MSP), which initiated drives to collect clothing, books, and money to send in support of the brave people who were literally risking their lives in the freedom rides and sit-ins. I was involved in MSP, and after being appointed dean of academic affairs I helped to create RILEEH, a program of cooperation involving the university, Rust College in Holly Springs, Mississippi, and LeMoyne College in Memphis. We applied for and received funds for the project from the federal government under Title III of the Higher Education Act of 1965.

Rust College in particular caught the attention and affection of people in Iowa. Its excellent choir had given concerts during annual tours through Iowa, Nebraska, and South Dakota, but the school had not been accredited. Ninety percent of Rust College students came from families with annual incomes below $2,000, so it was the only feasible college opportunity for the sons and daughters of many poverty-stricken Mississippi families. We arranged for student exchanges, brought their business managers to the university for internships with our business office, and enrolled members of the faculty for summer courses in their respective fields. After eight years of such cooperation, Rust College gained accreditation, some of its graduates enrolled at the University of Iowa for graduate study, and some of them stayed to work. Iowa was making a difference in the larger world. A more complete report of the RILEEH program is reprinted as an appendix in the book *New Dawns*.

My work with RILEEH proved to be much more than an administrative assignment, because it introduced me to a different culture — a closed society. I could see firsthand how an oppressive majority sacrificed its own spiritual and economic health for the dubious privilege of maintaining its advantage over an almost helpless minority. It also introduced me to some warm and wonderful people who gratefully accepted our offer of assistance and carried on very effectively after they had turned the corner and saw a new dawn of hope and opportunity.

Good-bye to In Loco Parentis

Although my work with RILEEH was an early priority after being appointed dean of academic affairs because someone needed to coordinate the developments already under way, my principal responsibility was to bring the student services into closer harmony with the heart of the university's operation — the colleges and the academic programs. As I gained experience in the new position, two primary themes began to emerge: improving the quality of the undergraduate experience, and bringing students with nontraditional backgrounds into the university who could succeed if given adequate academic and financial support. These goals were sometimes described as excellence and accessibility.

Some of the university's basic characteristics needed revision before we could work effectively toward our long-range goals, and the new position was symbolic of the university's determination to intervene decisively to bring about change. My position appeared to fulfill my desires to apply my academic experience in matters central to the mission of universities, to work in a larger arena in the cause of human rights, and to have a long-range effect, since the university and city communities adopted the national emphasis on civil rights. I proceeded with enthusiasm, and with Boyd providing primary leadership, the university modified its operations to support more directly the cause of human rights for students, faculty, and staff in the university community as well as for people at a distance.

My remarks in an interview by Phyllis Fleming of the *Cedar Rapids Gazette* in December 1965 give some insight into my feelings at that time.

> It is unusual for an engineer to go this far astray. For several years I've emphasized that what we (engineers) do influences our civilization, our culture, and whether we are to be destroyed. An engineer should be concerned with the social consequences of his work. We can't just be concerned with the end. We have to be involved at the elementary level of planning. . . . When the opportunity (to be dean) was presented, I thought "you've been insisting on this so here is the chance. What are you going to do?" . . . My life hasn't been based on doing the safe thing.

Soon after my appointment, Boyd directed me to resign from my faculty position on the board in control of athletics. I had enjoyed that assignment not only because the board exerted a substantial influence on an important part of the student body, but I must confess that I also enjoyed the generous perquisites. These included tickets for the entire family for all home games (many seats were empty in those days — for example, basketball ticket holders could remain at no added cost for the ensuing wrestling meets, and schoolchildren could sit in the end-zone football seats for fifty cents); travel with the football team to one game away from home each season; and gourmet meals at each meeting of the board. Boyd proceeded to eliminate the perks not only for the athletics board, but for other advisory committees, on the principle that no special reward should be expected for performing a regular faculty service.

My appointment to a position in the central university inspired the usual flurry of interviews and news articles, and in one such interview a student writer for the *Daily Iowan* was intrigued by the fact that Chris was born on Christmas day. The Christmas season was approaching, so he made her the centerpiece of his article. In the December 1, 1966, issue he wrote:

"Christmas day to the Hubbards also means an oaken yule log in the fireplace, presents and a meal of Christ's favorite foods, including roast beef and German chocolate cake." The blooper was picked up by the *New Yorker* magazine in its little endnotes, so Chris got national coverage for her nineteenth birthday. Peter's art class received national publicity because their very creative teacher had them paint a mural on the construction fence near their school, and a photo of the class at work was widely distributed.

As dean of academic affairs, my principal responsibility was to supervise the operation of the following university-level student-service offices: admissions, registrar, residence services, student financial aids, university counseling service, examination and evaluation service, Hancher Auditorium, Iowa Memorial Union, university placement service, Women's Resource and Action Center, campus programs and student activities, dean of students, office of cooperative education, special support services, and the Old Capitol Museum. Some of the offices were not a part of my original responsibilities; in fact, some of them were created during my tenure as the university's priorities changed. The student health service operated under the supervision of the university hospital, but I included its director in staff meetings of the student service directors so that we could benefit from his or her advice on student matters.

The office of recreational services was one of my original responsibilities, and its director, Harry Ostrander, worked very effectively with an advisory committee chaired by student Dan Pomeroy. We developed plans to convert the fieldhouse to purely recreational use after the completion of Carver Hawkeye Arena, which could accommodate the intercollegiate programs formerly held in the Fieldhouse. In the course of preparing for the remodeling, the architects discovered that ad hoc construction of handball courts had so overloaded the roof trusses that they were in danger of collapsing, so the building had to be vacated until the problem was corrected. To obtain better coordination with the athletic programs with the new facilities in operation, responsibility for the recreation program was transferred to the vice president for finance and university services, then later to the vice president for university relations.

As an agent of the vice president for academic affairs, I was responsible for much more than student services; in fact, I would not have accepted a traditional position administering a system based on an obsolete concept. My responsibilities included an unusual involvement in strictly academic programs as well as promoting the role of the fine arts units. I chaired the original Council on Teaching for many years as well as the Iowa Center for the Arts from its creation in 1968 until I retired in 1991. The unusual number of offices was manageable because most of the administrators were willing to adopt change, worked well together, and were given leeway to innovate and otherwise use their experience. Even so, it would have been impossible without my principal colleague Phillip Jones, and office staffs headed by Ann K. Huntzinger and Belinda Marner. My highly competent personal secretaries were Karen Knowling Albertus, who I had known as a student in my Sunday school class, and Sherilyn Sorge.

Both Ann and Belinda started as my secretaries, but I promoted them to professional status because they had the skills to perform at a higher level. It was difficult to gain promotions from general staff to professional classification because such promotions had been used by some administrators merely to reward secretaries who had reached the salary limit in their pay grade. Mary Jo Small, the administrator who oversaw the personnel office, happened to be located in the same suite I occupied, and she watched carefully to assure that I had indeed elevated Ann's duties to the professional level. Ann performed so well that incoming president James Freedman later asked her to head his office staff, and Rawlings, the next president, asked her to stay. When he resigned to become president of Cornell University, he convinced her to run his office there. Belinda is now assistant vice president for student services.

I viewed my immediate staff as family more than subordinates. Ann and her family have been my friends for many years; I attended her wedding to Alvon, and brought little gifts to Lori and Lisa when I returned from business trips. I remember that Lisa was born on the day that Mount St. Helens erupted, but I never blamed Ann for triggering that event. When I retired, Belinda worked with the office of university relations to compile big notebook of clippings and documents that have been an invaluable asset as I write these memoirs. She and Sherry still remember my birthdays, and provide any help that I need to locate records.

My experience as a professor in a technical field and lack of training in student affairs led to an unorthodox tenure as chief student personnel administrator. I had not taken any of the courses in the student personnel curriculum, and had only a vague notion of what counselors did. My general approach for administering the ongoing primary operations was the same as I would have used for a technical problem — consult experts in the field, and hire competent administrators. Finding experts was no problem, because Professor Albert Hood and some of his colleagues had national stature as student personnel administrators. Hood attended our staff meetings, one of his graduate students, Jim Dickinson, helped me as a half-time administrative assistant, and the heads of the various departments under my supervision were quite competent. Our primary goals were to change counselors' roles vis-à-vis students, to bring them into the mainstream of the university's mission rather than let them operate as if they were independent units, and to use space and staff to advance university priorities.

My deficiencies as an administrator went beyond an ignorance of the principles of counseling, so I talked to Boyd about attending a workshop for new academic administrators at Harvard. He suggested that I might be better served by studying a good book on management, and I proceeded to do so. I learned that the definition of management was "achieving a goal by directing the efforts of others." My engineering research and teaching had not been carried out through others, and my boyhood failure as a salesman was a warning that convincing people was not my forte. I found that the best procedure for me was to consult liberally with student government officers and relevant administrators and then present written plans to achieve university goals, rather than rely on administrators to present proposals to me. The technique worked well during a period of rapid change, and led to substantial revisions in the operation of residence halls and creation of the Iowa Center for the Arts and the office of special support services, for example. The RILEEH venture, the creation of undergraduate scholar assistantships, a mentoring program for at-risk students, and Opportunity at Iowa were created from whole cloth, then administered with a minimum of new personnel. The latter was important because existing staff resents the appointment of a new person to do what they could manage to do, and because I am not an empire builder (and perhaps not a good manager). Because I did not consciously try to direct the staff, I have been uncomfortable when someone refers me to as a leader. I merely developed plans, did my part, and expected others to do likewise.

My introduction to management was not free of serious difficulties. The director of admissions and the registrar were assigned to other duties when they complained to the president about my supervision, and the director of Iowa Memorial Union offered his resignation to the president as a matter of protest: it was accepted on the spot. I do not know the basis of their complaints, and did not ask. I soon fired the associate director of the Union for insubordination, and referred his lawyer to the university counsel when he appealed my decision. I also initiated formal proceedings that led to the dismissal of a senior staff member for violating the ethical code of his profession. I guess I wasn't a nice guy. I had excellent but often grudging cooperation from all the staff who continued in their positions, moving the student services from the traditional in loco parentis posture to a policy of treating students as adults with more personal freedom and commensurate responsibility for their behavior.

Searches for directors sometimes encountered difficulty because different relevant groups could not agree on the best candidate. When we interviewed applicants for director of admissions, one generally approved candidate withdrew because his teenage daughter liked field hockey and the Iowa City schools did not offer the sport. I didn't mind losing him. Colleagues in the colleges served by the admissions office were unanimous in support of Michael Barron from the University of Texas, but the office staff thought he was too brusque and might not work well with staff. I disagreed but could not ignore their reservations, so I asked Mike to meet with the staff to discuss their concerns before offering the position to him. He convinced them that his "Texas style" was consistent with a concern for all aspects of human rights, and I proceeded to appoint him. He performed so well that I gave him an annual raise even though his salary for the year was set by the negotiations preceding his appointment; I believe that it was an excellent investment.

The offices under my control included hundreds of full-time and part-time employees, and I had very little experience in personnel management. Incompetent or intransigent employees had been rare, and someone else had dealt with them. I could still leave most such problems to middle managers, but had direct responsibility for people reporting to me and for appeals from the decisions of the middle managers. I learned that a humane concern for the welfare of individual workers could conflict with the effective operation of an office, because managers sometimes gave an incompetent employee passing marks on annual personnel reviews to avoid a complaint or lawsuit. A subsequent action to discharge for failure to perform would be reversed on appeal because of an inadequate paper trail. The problem was aggravated still more when the manager would give a good recommendation to get rid of an incompetent employee who wanted to transfer to a position elsewhere.

Assembling a competent staff was important, but my primary concern was to move the student services forward in educational effectiveness. There were obstacles based on tradition to be overcome, including in loco parentis, which translates to "in the place of a parent," and student personnel administrators were the university's agents in that function. The policy affected a wide range of relationships among students, staff, and community. For example, unmarried undergraduate students were required to live in residence halls, with their parents, or in "approved" off-campus housing. Residence halls for women and men were on opposite sides of the river, visits by the opposite sex were strictly controlled, and unmarried undergraduate women had to observe a curfew in returning to their accommodations. They could not escape the requirements by living off campus because the landlords or landladies of such housing were required to enforce the rules as a condition for approval. A related parietal rule required undergraduates to live in residence halls for two reasons: the programs in the halls were considered to be important assets in the education of freshmen and sophomores in particular; and full occupancy was important for servicing the revenue bonds that financed the capital construction. It was seldom necessary to invoke the rule because enrollment grew so fast that space was not available to accommodate all of the students covered by the rule.

Students who had problems in the community were rescued or punished by staff in the Office of Student Affairs. Nonacademic administrators such as the dean of students or the director of the student health service could dismiss a student without faculty involvement if the administrator disapproved of the student's behavior. The dean of students rescued students who had been arrested for off-campus misdemeanors, with the understanding that he would take appropriate corrective action, and a student's registration could be canceled for nonpayment of rent to an off-campus landlord.

These are only a few examples of the very oppressive practices that were in place, all done with the cooperation of parents. In fact, when we began to change the policies, parents raised severe objections and registered formal complaints against the responsible administrators. I particularly remember an anonymous letter stating that the writer's original endorsement of my appointment had changed to disappointment because my support for coeducational living arrangements (that is, men and women on different floors of the same building) was inconsistent with what they had assumed were my moral values. That was an interesting point, because Chris was headed for a private college at the time and needed our permission to live in coeducational housing. Wynonna and I gave permission, but our uneasiness helped me to understand what other parents were experiencing.

As one might expect, students were among the most enthusiastic supporters for change, and it was difficult to avoid being in the middle of family disputes. Since students and parents were equally important from an administrative viewpoint, we adopted a procedure to keep students fully informed of any change through my weekly meetings with officers of the student government and consulting legal counsel to assure compliance with relevant laws. When a controversial change was under consideration, students were offered options to live under new rules, or to choose accommodations where the old in loco parentis rules were enforced. The choice was part of the regular contract signed by students and parents. The procedure removed us from the middle of family disputes, but many parents resented having to make the decision. A vanishing minority of students chose to live in closely regulated accommodations, and the university accepted the continuing responsibility to enforce the contract for such students. I always spoke formally to parents when they visited the campus for the orientation of incoming students, giving them an opportunity to express worries about the university's influence on the students' values. My response was that our responsibility was to place new information at the disposal of students and teach them how to analyze, not to indoctrinate them. Parents might be concerned about some of the ideas expressed by their offspring during the undergraduate years, but extensive research showed that the college experience involved much questioning of traditional assumptions, and finally tended to reinforce the values with which they entered. With regard to what parents should do, my answer was, "Love them and trust them; four years of questioning and exploring will not erase your influence during the first eighteen years of their lives."

Sandy and I frequently consulted David Vernon, professor and former dean of the law school, as we developed new policies related to human rights, casting off the remnants of in loco parentis, or dealing with protests. He was always calm and thoughtful, and his Solomon-like advice taught me a great deal about human behavior. For example, I had been proceeding on the assumption that students were not only academically talented but also were well above average in ethical behavior. He warned me that such an assumption is not only questionable as a matter of fact, but also that it was not a sound basis for making policy. In nonacademic attributes, students are pretty much like other people in their age group. I now realize that he was correct in his advice, but somehow I still feel that students are special people. We benefited even more from his wisdom when he was appointed to the position of provost.

We brought parents into the process of change by seeking their advice on matters they considered important at the fall orientation of students or on other occasions when they visited the campus. Not satisfied with a passive approach, I initiated a project, supported by the Parents Association, to call the parents of all freshmen outside of Johnson County (to keep the numbers manageable) about two months after the beginning of fall term. The callers were students employed for the task and were given a script for the interviews. After a quick explanation to assure the parent that we were not selling something and that their offspring was not in trouble, parents were asked if their son or daughter (callers used the name of the son or daughter) was receiving the experience they had expected. Parents were grateful to know that someone at the large and ostensibly impersonal university cared, and the response was usually favorable. When problems were identified, the information was given to me and I personally contacted the person in the university who could help the student and arranged an appointment for the two of them to meet. My secretary kept accurate records close at hand, so I could respond quickly when a parent called to explain a problem further, to thank us for solving it, or perhaps to see if a vice president really was interested in their student's problems. The public relations staff enthusiastically endorsed the program, and handled the administrative details associated with employing the student callers and setting up the bank of telephones. As a bonus, I became acquainted with the officers of the Parents Association and include them among the many friends I have met through the university.

The program was not merely a palliative for parents, however: a student's problem often disclosed a deficiency in the university operation, and remedial steps were then taken by correcting individual staff errors, revising staff training, or changing policies where necessary. I wonder if that type of "counseling" is taught in the counseling profession, or if the objective of counselors is to help the client adjust to the rules of the institution, even though the rules may be flawed or a staff member may be at fault. Perhaps my lack of counselor training was not altogether a handicap.

Removing unnecessary restrictions on students was important, but we had to guard against people who tried to exploit the inexperience of thousands of trusting young people in a captive situation. Security against theft and assault was a major concern, and the security force was expanded to protect students. Sometimes the exploitation was more subtle, however: for example, we found that merchants of cooking utensils and tableware would have a "party" in a woman student's room, similar to vendors' parties in private homes, where the "hostess" invited friends and neighbors, and the vendor would sign up purchasers. Students who were not engaged or otherwise planning to establish a home would end up with large boxes of utensils or dishes in a crowded room, and with hundreds of dollars of debt. We denied the vendors access to the residence halls and told them that they could rent a hotel room off campus for their "parties."

Financial management was another area where students pressed for control over the mandatory activity fees. The fees were allocated by committees including faculty and administrators, who exerted a considerable influence. Since the fees, once approved, were imposed on all students, they felt that allocation decisions should be theirs entirely. Consistent with our changed view of students as adults rather than minors needing parental supervision, a procedure was negotiated for the elected student government to make decisions on the distribution of activity fees with the regents' approval, with the stipulation that the university would control the actual disbursement as its fiduciary responsibility.

The Public Interest Research Groups inspired by Ralph Nader presented a much more difficult problem than the "parties" because their standard tactic to raise money was an "opt-out fee" imposed on all students under the authority of the student government. A fee dedicated to the Iowa Public Interest Research Group (IPIRG) was put on every student's university account with proceeds going to IPIRG, and those who did not want to pay could opt out by notifying the business office. Some students objected to this tactic, but the student government was reluctant to change it because the substantial income was controlled by managers they selected, and was used for political lobbying. When we suggested that students "opt in" rather than "opt out," the student government disagreed because the difference amounted to many thousands of dollars: students who did not want to pay didn't bother to request an exemption. We believed that this tax on apathy was inconsistent with the best interests of students, and insisted on the "opt-in" fee over the strong opposition of the student government. Because the practice was used at all three of the state universities, the final decision to "opt in" was made by the regents.

Our plans for the residence halls were not merely to remove the restrictions of in loco parentis, but to use the staff and facilities to augment academic programs and to advance other university priorities. Reserve library stations equipped with the materials most used by lower-division students, music practice rooms, tutoring carrels, study rooms, and computer terminals were placed in the residence halls. Students were encouraged to use their guest meal tickets to invite faculty members and administrators to dinner, and they received special discounts to purchase tickets for performances in Hancher Auditorium. Such programs to improve educational value were made in consultation with advisory committees of students, faculty, and student service administrators, with enthusiastic cooperation from directors Ted Rehder and George Droll and the residence hall staff. An unplanned benefit was that more students lived in the residence halls for a longer time. Students living in the halls also supported the university's efforts to recruit a more diverse student body, and their cooperation helped to orient students from nontraditional backgrounds and increased the interaction among various ethnic groups.

Traditionally, the student housing operation had been the business vice president's responsibility, and the use of space and staff reflected the priorities of a business manager. The director of the residence hall system and his senior staff were located in the building with the central business office, occupying space that would be needed for the growing academic programs. The salaries of the resident staff in the halls were supported from the general education fund, which improved the balance sheet for the financial operations and provided more space for student rooms. Subsidies from the general education fund were desirable because they helped keep housing fees at a relatively low level, but the regents reluctantly decided to discontinue the subsidies in view of the unmet needs of the academic programs for which the general fund was the primary support. The director and his staff were relocated to space in a residence hall, and salaries for the resident advisers were shifted to the residence hall budgets. Similar policies had been used at the other regents universities, and they ordered the removal of the subsidy at all three over a period of several years, thereby freeing funds for internal reallocation. I used those funds to support the academic programs described above, strengthen other student services, correct salary inequities, and help the public service programs in the Iowa Center for the Arts.

Although I was not familiar with the term at that time, my technique was to use a form of zero-base budgeting. The basic programs were carried forward automatically at budgeting time, but new or reallocated funds were treated as a lump sum that could be allocated in accordance with priorities established in consultation with other administrators and the regents. At the annual time for preparing new budgets, I was the despair of the accounting department, which usually shifted funds in units, or lines. When I simply eliminated entire programs and funded new ones, they had trouble tracing the lines. After they concluded that my procedures were legitimate though unorthodox, we got along just fine.

The state legislature and the governor chronically failed to appropriate funds for the regents' category of "institutional improvement," and my process for managing resources moved the university forward. When that source was denied, I used internal reallocation to fund programs that had been approved through the normal channels up through the regents. These included programs to promote cultural diversity, to remedy salary inequities, to support summer programs designed for women, and to fund the undergraduate scholar assistantships described earlier. Substantially increased funding for student financial aid was also a high priority need because when the subsidies were eliminated, rates for residence halls had to be raised, and the restrictions in state allocations required us to raise the tuition. This was a serious problem because we wanted to accommodate many more students from lower-income families. The solution reached by the regents was to set aside a portion of the total tuition for student aid to supplement the regular allocation. This had the net effect that students from higher-income families outside of Iowa were paying essentially the full cost of their education, while the state allocation subsidized the cost for resident students, especially those with lower income.

I especially appreciated the assistance of the women who created the Women's Resource and Action Center (WRAC), because they initiated and executed programs that I as a male could never have conceived and operated. They helped the university to extend educational opportunity to women with nontraditional backgrounds and assist them through the often difficult problems of attitudinal barriers, housing, child-care needs, refuge from abuse, and abortion counseling. In my view, many of the problems faced by women are created by the cruelty of some men and by the failure of men to accept their responsibility as partners, and I am proud to have supported the establishment and continuing operation of the Rape Victim Advocacy Program (RVAP). I extend my deepest gratitude to Mary Cooper, Linda McGuire, Susan Buckley, Maria (Papusa) Molina, and Monique DiCarlo, who served as directors of WRAC during my tenure, and to Karla Miller, who founded RVAP.

Applications for admission to the university were another problem from the perspective of human rights, because they requested information about race, religion, family income, alumni in the family, and other data that were not necessary to make a decision on admissibility. We changed the forms so that the required information was reduced to a minimum — academic credentials, name, address, and telephone number, with optional information about race and gender. Additional information was requested *after* applicants had been informed of their admission.

In working with the office of admissions, I learned much about the way high school students and their parents viewed the university, and the effectiveness with which high schools prepared students for the challenges of college. When the state director of education ordered a consolidation of the high schools to obtain classes large enough to offer the courses necessary for success in college, many communities reacted in highly negative fashion. They apparently viewed the schools from the aspect of community identity and sports teams rather than as preparing students for successful lives. The regents came to the director's aid by requiring more preparation in English, science, and mathematics for admission to the state universities, with a four-year period allowed for the school districts to make the necessary adjustment in their curricula. The increased requirements were not inspired by the desire to consolidate schools, but were in response to widespread faculty complaints that students simply were not prepared for the demands of college work. There were major deficiencies in students' understanding of science and mathematics and in their ability to write standard English. Students complained to me about the deficiencies in their high schools; one was so unhappy that she went to a meeting of her hometown school board to inform them that she was handicapped by inadequate preparation in spite of having taken all of the courses offered in her school.

John Moore, who was director of student financial aid when I was appointed, took on the added responsibility for the admissions office when its director resigned, and served admirably in that capacity until he retired. He and the admissions staff found that former athletes and coaches were some of the most effective recruiters because they were in tune with people in some of the smaller communities. Former high school coach Howard Vernon visited most of the high schools in Iowa as a very effective representative of the university office of admissions, and later became principal of City High. Dick Schultz, former head coach of the Hawkeye basketball team, developed summer sports camps as a representative of the admissions office, and later was appointed executive director of the U.S. Olympic Committee. The idea of summer sports camps was a master stroke supported by Executive Vice President George Chambers, because the camps have provided many students with a favorable college experience and gave them an opportunity to participate in campus activities in addition to their chosen sport. Of course, the athletic coaches were very pleased by the extra income and the opportunity to contact future candidates for their intercollegiate teams.

The presidents during my tenure did not enter office as enthusiastic supporters of athletics, but quickly learned that their goals for the academic programs and facilities could be achieved more readily by channeling some of the public enthusiasm for sports into support for other programs. For example, when Roy Carver wanted to provide artificial turf for the football stadium, Boyd accepted with thanks and discussed with Carver some of his other goals for the university. Carver was very receptive, and eventually provided funds for the Museum of Art, endowed professorships, and the Educational Opportunity Program. Sandy was sharply criticized by some fans when he responded to complaints about our record in sports by observing that we had the best art museum in the Big Ten. When the public demand for a basketball arena rose to a fever pitch, he insisted that its construction should not drain resources from the general fund that supports the academic programs. The University of Iowa Foundation came to his aid by launching a capital campaign to turn public enthusiasm into financial support, and the necessary money was raised so quickly that our eyes were opened to an untapped source for many university programs. Carver provided the major gift for the private campaign, and Carver Hawkeye Arena bears his name.

Incoming president James O. Freedman was quite experienced in private fund-raising, and urged the university to launch a major capital campaign for endowed professorships, doctoral fellowships, and human academic resources, rather than for "bricks and mortar." Our experience with the arena funding was repeated, and the goal was reached so quickly that it was expanded. Our subsequent success in private fund-raising has supported substantial gains in the academic quality of the university. The public enthusiasm for sports entertainment is not entirely responsible for the course of events, but it is a genuine asset as we pursue our academic goals.

Hunter Rawlings had been a star basketball center and baseball pitcher in his undergraduate years at Haverford College, and hence had the perspective of player and professor. That did not protect him from the wrath of coaches and alumni when he proposed that students not participate in intercollegiate contests until their sophomore year. When the national college organizations declined to act on the idea, Rawlings commented that Iowa might adopt the rule unilaterally. At this suggestion, fans and coaches virtually went into orbit, and football coach Hayden Fry threatened to resign. We probably would have encountered less public criticism if a president had suggested eliminating the Department of Classics, in which Rawlings was a professor.

I was especially pleased with results from the Educational Opportunity program (EOP), created in 1968, because it is an excellent example of the impact the university has had on the larger society. EOP was established in honor of Dr. Martin Luther King Jr., and its first director was Phillip E. Jones, an alumnus who returned to the university from his teaching position in Flint, Michigan, to accept the responsibility. His assigned mission was to reach out to the low-income ethnic minority populations whose representation in the student body was grossly disproportionate to their presence in the general population.

Unofficial estimates are that 146 African American students were enrolled in 1965. Although the records do not specify which students were of Latino, American Indian, or Asian ancestry, it is generally accepted that they were few in number; their representation had been no greater and was probably much less than that of African Americans. Under the leadership of Dr. Jones, the enrollment of minorities grew rapidly from an initial EOP class of forty-two undergraduates in fall 1968 to a total of 971 minority Americans in an overall enrollment of 22,766 in 1987.

Students in the first EOP class proceeded to demonstrate the value of the program. Percy Watson, a freshman from Hattiesburg, Mississippi, was elected to Phi Beta Kappa, graduated in three years, completed law school, practiced in Alaska, and returned to his native Mississippi where he practices law and has been elected and reelected five times to the state legislature. His classmate from Mississippi, Donald Russell, subsequently earned the M.D. degree at the University of Maryland, was certified in the ear, nose, and throat specialty, and returned to practice in Gulfport, Mississippi. Cornelius Thornton from South Chicago was admitted on recommendation of a community counselor in spite of an abysmal academic record in high school, and he proceeded to graduate with distinction, earn the M.B.A. degree at the University of Chicago, and advance to the position of vice president, investment research department, Goldman Sachs and Company.

Several of the students in the original EOP class were graduates of Central High School in Kansas City, and those who came to Iowa were especially energetic and creative, initiating the Black Genesis Dance Troupe and assuming leadership roles in general. One of them, Mae Colleen Thompson, made an excellent record, earned the B.B.A. at Iowa, and was appointed to succeed Phillip Jones as director of the office of special support services. After serving capably, she proceeded to earn the master's degree at the University of Southern California and a doctorate in business administration at George Washington University. She married Melvin Jones of Memphis, another member of the same class. Melvin graduated in 1972, and was appointed Iowa City budget director. His career has included chief financial officer for the District of Columbia, vice president and treasurer of Howard University, and a Ph.D. in public finance from George Washington University. Colleen and Mel are now at the University of Nebraska–Lincoln; she is professor of business administration, and he is vice president for finance. These are but a few of the hundreds of minority graduates from EOP programs in all academic areas who have made important contributions to our society. Their success illustrates the truth of the slogan "a mind is a terrible thing to waste," because many of these successes would not have occurred without the existence of a special opportunity.

As the minority student population grew, they demanded changes in the culture of the university community and courses of study, leading to the establishment of the Afro-American Cultural Center and the Chicano/American Indian Cultural Center. At the same time, women students demanded changes to meet their needs, and I assisted them in creating and staffing the Women's Resource and Action Center, all in university-owned houses allocated for the purpose. Each group demanded that courses of study in their respective history and culture be established. I was appointed to chair a committee to create a course in Afro-American studies, and professor of English Robert Corrigan was appointed secretary. He was the real expert on African American studies, but the tenor of the times was against a white person heading the academic program. The course was duly created in the Program in American Studies, nationally recognized African American scholar Charles Davis was recruited to chair the program, and it eventually evolved into a full-fledged interdisciplinary program of African American World Studies offering degrees at all levels, now headed by Professor William Welburn. A similar process was used to create a program in women's studies, which is much larger in scope.

When Freedman succeeded Boyd as president in 1982, he was impressed by the self-effacing attitude of the university toward student quality and fund-raising capability. At his urging, a campaign to raise $100 million by the year 2000 was launched, and the goal was reached so quickly that the limit was raised to

$150 million; the total has now reached $240 million. Freedman was impressed by the high quality of Iowa students, and urged us to promote their prospects for graduate scholarships and fellowships, and to recruit yet more freshmen with outstanding credentials.

A Presidential Scholarship program had been established in 1979 for students whose high school achievements and standard test scores were outstanding. It successfully attracted students with exceptional qualifications, using traditional criteria, but it was soon evident that excellent applicants with exceptional ability in the fine arts were passed over because the conventional selection criteria omitted any measure of their greatest strengths. Similarly, our regular recruitment practices failed to reach the best-qualified minority applicants. Awards equivalent to the Presidential Scholarships were then created to attract a more balanced class; Iowa Center for the Arts Scholarships and Minority Achievement Scholarships. Applicants in the performing arts were auditioned by the relevant faculty, and applicants in the visual arts submitted portfolios. Minority applicants were recruited from the National Achievement semifinalists. The new awards were successful in attracting excellent applicants, and I made telephone calls to encourage the enrollment of minority applicants who were selected by the admissions staff and faculty in related areas. Njeri Fuller, one of the minority scholars, was invited to deliver the student address at her commencement, and referred to my telephone call as one of the reasons she enrolled at Iowa.

We believed that the students enrolled under the University Scholars program could best achieve their full potential through supplementing traditional academic programs. At this highest level of student aptitude, President James Garfield's remark in a speech to Williams College alumni seemed especially appropriate: "Give me a log hut with only a simple bench, Mark Hopkins on one end and I on the other, and you may have all the buildings, apparatus and libraries without him." To me, that meant calling on the university's crown jewels, the faculty; they are the asset that distinguish universities from other educational institutions such as libraries and museums. I then designed a program the university eventually created, undergraduate scholar assistantships, or simply USAs, to be awarded to students whose academic records placed them in the top 1 percent of all undergraduates. The assistantship enabled them to work individually with tenured or tenure-track professors of their choice in significant projects of teaching, research, and creative scholarship. USAs were automatically offered to the students in the University Scholarship programs described above. Modest stipends roughly equal to resident tuition were provided. Neither the mentor nor the project needed to be in the area of the student's academic major, so that an engineering student could work with a music professor, for example. Traditional criteria for measuring achievement — grades and scores on standardized tests — were used to select "late bloomers," and provisions were made to accommodate nominations by faculty members whose personal experience confirmed that the candidate was performing at a level in the top 1 percent of all students they had known.

Outreach, admission, and financial and academic support for all undergraduates were included in my responsibilities as dean of academic affairs, and special attention to nontraditional students was a high priority for the university in the midst of a nationwide concern for civil rights. The Educational Opportunity program, created in 1968 and headed by Phillip Jones, had very encouraging success in reaching out to nontraditional families, and the enrollment of minority students increased by an order of magnitude in the period between 1968 and 1987. Our success was less than we desired, and we quickly concluded that contact with nontraditional students must be made long before the usual time of the junior year in high school. That was far too late, because the typical low-income student had not taken the courses needed to enter and succeed in college. I was the original director of the Upward Bound program funded under Title III of the Higher Education Act of 1965 to support low-income and minority students in the tenth, eleventh, and twelfth grades in cooperation with high school teachers, counselors, and administrators.

As the university gained experience with Upward Bound, we learned that a still earlier intervention was required to help nontraditional students and their families with skill development, motivation, and information about the relationship between education and their economic future. With strong support from the state board of regents, we conceived and implemented the Opportunity at Iowa program to provide academic counseling and financial support for low-income and minority students, beginning in elementary school. The program was a high-priority project for me, and I served as director of Opportunity at Iowa until I retired.

Development of Opportunity at Iowa began with a half-day retreat on October 1, 1987, at the president's house on Church Street. Interim president Richard Remington had invited the vice presidents, the deans of the colleges, the director of affirmative action, the director of libraries, and the dean of students to explore ways to implement the directive of the regents to increase minority enrollment. Related goals involving makeup of the faculty and staff and the content of academic programs were included in the discussion, and I served by default as reporter for the group, took notes, and turned to the challenge of integrating their ideas into a practical program — a typical challenge for an engineer! Not so typical was waking up in the wee hours of the next morning to the cadence of a wordless quatrain resounding in my head — almost wordless, because the final part was three words that summarized our discussion: Seek the Best.

Experience told me that returning to slumber would not be possible until the cadence was endowed with words, so I began to write on the pad I always kept by my bed. Using a nest as a metaphor for the university, I found that after my first and only poem emerged, sleep again became possible.

> If one would amass a wealth of minds
> to serve as the idea's nest,
> Then walk the world of humankind
> and for the aerie seek only the best.

The poem needed an appropriate setting, and an allegorical journey to excellence appeared as the vehicle. After lively discussions at weekly meetings of the president's "docket group" or cabinet, I blended the twin values of excellence and human rights into a document which was duly approved by the representative assemblies of faculty, students, and staff, and by the state board of regents. The document outlined reasons to obtain a more balanced representation of the total population of minority students and incorporate them more completely into the university community. It is reproduced as appendix B in *New Dawns*.

When the fall semester began in 1994, 741 African Americans, 95 American Indians, 1,038 Asian Americans, and 539 Hispanic Americans were enrolled. The total of 2,413 minority students was 9.0 percent of the university total of 26,932, so that the Opportunity at Iowa goal of 8.5 percent had been exceeded. Comparable figures for the fall of 1995 were 2,537, or 9.2 percent minority students in a total enrollment of 27,597.

Encouragement of women to pursue careers in nontraditional fields was an early priority for me, and I was a founding member of the Society of Women Engineers at the university. The College of Engineering is now a national leader in the enrollment of women, and the number of women in the professional colleges of business, dentistry, law, and medicine has increased from less than 10 percent in 1970 to well over one-third in 1996. The College of Pharmacy has had the most dramatic growth — from 11 percent in 1940 to 31 percent in 1970 to 65 percent in 1995. I also advocated the appointment of women to faculty positions in all colleges, and testified in 1988 on behalf of legislation to support more minorities and women, which resulted in the Regents' Minority and Women Educators Enhancement Act. The funds thus appropriated were allocated by the provost to encourage searches for women by offering salary supplements to departments that successfully recruited women in certain faculty positions.

Assembling a staff and developing programs was guided by a concern for human rights and the associated principle of affirmative action. Has affirmative action demonstrated its value to the degree that it should be continued indefinitely? Although white males were in the majority among the administrators I appointed, the proportion of women and minorities was relatively high for several reasons: an insistence on quality, the character of a university, and a university policy on affirmative action.

Our nationwide searches for people to fill the more senior positions produced a substantial number of women and minority candidates who were "overqualified" in their current positions; discriminatory hiring and promotion in their past had the interesting effect of enriching the proportion of well-qualified women and minorities in the hiring pool. Comparing qualifications based on educational background and years of experience, they were at less senior ranks than white male candidates with similar backgrounds, and the lower rank was a negative element when using traditional criteria of quality for evaluation. If quality was our primary goal, then the vicious cycle had to be interrupted. Moreover, unfair discrimination has deprived most minority persons and many women of the *opportunity* to gain the necessary education and experience, and it is unreasonable to penalize the victims for the resulting deficiencies.

The character of universities relates to their primary mission of preparing students for successful operation in their society and in the larger world. American society is equally divided between men and women, and has a rapidly increasing proportion of ethnic minorities, estimated to reach 50 percent during the lifetime of today's students. Successful operation in such an environment requires a knowledge and hopefully an appreciation of the world's diversity. Failure to understand other cultures should not limit a student's progress, and stresses that inevitably arise in any society can be relieved effectively without resort to oppressive measures. The required understanding is impossible to achieve if the representation of women and minorities in the academic community is well below the national proportion or if they are only in stereotypical positions. Nor can understanding be achieved through academia alone or by depending on mass media to provide the information. Students must see an accurate balance in their academic environment and should be encouraged to interact intellectually with people who are different from themselves and others in their experience. Achieving the necessary environment is therefore a legitimate component of educational quality.

Affirmative action enters the picture at this point because the vicious cycle cannot be interrupted without taking all the factors into account. First, educational and employment opportunities must be extended to minorities and women so that their innate talents can be fully developed; second, the search net must be expanded to reach nontraditional populations; finally, when they have the necessary qualifications, minorities and women should be hired and promoted. These are the elements of affirmative action, despite attempts in some quarters to distort them into a "straw man" of "quotas" that can be handily demolished. I believe that these elements have been observed in filling the positions listed above, and note that no complaints have been received from candidates who were not chosen. Critics who claim that affirmative action is equivalent to quotas usually refer to the targets that have been adopted, often in exasperation, when employers persistently avoid the intent of the law by rationalizing the appointment of white males after going through the motion of affirmation action procedures.

For seven years I was a member and later chaired the board of visitors for General Motors Institute (GMI) in Flint, Michigan, a degree-granting institution that was then a division of General Motors. The experience was especially significant because I learned how a giant "hard-nosed" corporation can use its resources to achieve a goal that is not only in its best interest but also serves as an example to employers who complain about the burden of affirmative action. The directors and top executives surveyed the company's personnel, market, and locations and concluded that corporate interests would be best served by substantial increases in the numbers of minorities and women at all levels. The move enabled them to upgrade their workforce, helped the communities where they were located, and provided some of their prime customers with income to purchase their products. GMI serves as a major source of technical and management personnel for the corporation, with graduates in key positions right up to president. By recruiting and supporting substantial increases in the enrollment of regularly admissible minorities and women, they produced a steady flow of well-qualified employees to meet the corporate goal. That is affirmative action at its best, and might be compared with the bombastic behavior and stonewalling of self-serving politicians and short-sighted employers who see affirmative action only as "social engineering."

Regarding the future of affirmation action, I recall conversations with Phil Jones and Pete Bryant during the early development of the Educational Opportunity and Upward Bound programs. We agreed that the ideal outcome of our efforts would be to make the programs unnecessary because the high schools had corrected the deficiencies that led to graduates who were unprepared for college work. The same hope could be applied to affirmative action programs: if employers and educational institutions were to adopt recruitment, training, and promotion policies based strictly on merit, there would be no need for programs that target neglected groups for special assistance. Utopia has not yet arrived in educational institutions or in employment practices, so both justice and the search for excellence demand that remedial policies continue.

Student Turbulence

My appointment to the university administration happened to coincide with the national protest movement on college campuses, and Iowa students joined in with enthusiasm (honest, I didn't put them up to it). The protests were the trial by fire that comprised my extraordinary initiation into academic administration. Many students had been active in the civil rights movement, and they basically viewed the Vietnam War as a violation of the human rights of the Vietnamese people by an external power. The level of protest escalated dramatically when the threat of being drafted reminded students that their own human rights were also in danger. They accused the university of complicity in the violation because we trained army and air force officers in ROTC and offered placement services to the Marine Corps and Dow Chemical company, manufacturer of the napalm that was used in Vietnam. The protests soon involved so many students and disrupted the normal operations of the university so seriously that many central university officials, including Vice Presidents Boyd and Spriestersbach and myself, had to devote our energy to maintain at least a semblance of order.

Throughout my administrative tenure, I met weekly with officers of the student government to exchange information and to share responsibility and authority. During the protest period, however, I spent much of my time meeting with the officers and protest leaders to channel their energy into tactics that supported their rights to free speech and free association while permitting the university to perform its primary mission — the education of *all* of its students. They tried to close the university as a statement of support for liberty, and we could not convince the leaders that a university closed by coercion would be a symbol of defeat, not victory, for freedom and democracy. My task was somewhat less difficult because the students sensed that my actions were directed toward the tactics they used rather than criticizing their values. At the beginning of the protests, my experience during World War II (a "just" war), when draft evasion was illegal and relatively rare, led me to take a dim view of their protests. As information came in about the rationale for the war and the way it was carried out, I became more sympathetic to the protesters' views but refrained from encouraging them. Tactics included breaking windows on campus and in downtown stores, bomb and arson threats, stopping traffic on the interstate highway, and launching bricks and bottles from a large hidden catapult into a major intersection. I pointed out the inconsistency of protesting on behalf of a distant group of people by abusing people close at hand, but they were not persuaded by my arguments. Some examples will illustrate the character of the demonstrations.

Jerry Sies came to the university as a freshman, and was soon noted for his creative freelance protest style. He delighted in tormenting administrators, led sit-ins in President Bowen's office, and became a frequent presence at Sandy's. I sometimes wondered if Bowen went to Claremont to escape Jerry's badgering. After Sandy became president, Jerry saw a work of art made by one of Sandy's children in elementary school. The weathered board studded with pebbles caused Jerry to regard Sandy in a new light: a president who exhibited such simple art in his office couldn't be *all* bad. That did not deter Jerry from his pranks, however. Somehow, he managed to present false documents certifying his eligibility for a degree, and his name duly appeared on the graduation roster. As I recall, he returned the diploma without a fuss because he only wanted to embarrass the administrators. He was mischievous, but not dishonest.

In contrast to the individualistic sniping of Sies, the well-organized Jim Sutton was easily elected president of the student government and used the position to demand a much greater role for students in institutional governance. He wanted to add students to all university committees and create a joint student-faculty senate with policymaking power. His very effective political style quickly caught the attention of state senator Francis Messerly, who insisted that anyone advocating overthrow of the democratic form of government be excluded from the campus. He missed the point of SDS and the other demonstrators — that the university governance was undemocratic. The intrusion of Messerly and other politicians into university governance was an ominous sign, and may have been the most damaging effect of the student protests. Sutton continued and expanded on his political activities after he graduated and became a lobbyist for the unionization of all state university employees.

Threats of bombing or arson were common tactics to harass administrators, and a bomb actually exploded in a trash can in front of the Civic Center in the wee hours of one night. A temporary building (Old Pink, for its color) housing the rhetoric program burned down under suspicious circumstances, but the fire marshal eventually decided that the fire was of electrical origin. Special measures were taken to protect university property: faculty volunteers stood watch in academic buildings through the night, and the regular glass in certain windows was replaced with shatter-resistant plastic. Small fires were set on campus, so a ban on fires was declared. The protesters then accused us of inconsistency; burning the homecoming monument on the Pentacrest was a campus tradition, and they exulted when we decided to be consistent and not burn the monument. I was especially unhappy because I hoped to retain many traditions to maintain a sense of continuity during a period of rapid change, some of our own making and others occurring in spite of our efforts. For decades, the monuments had been constructed by engineering students, using designs submitted in annual competitions that were usually won by students in the art department.

Protest actions quickly spread from the university campus to adjacent businesses that were judged by the protesters to be part of the establishment supporting the war. Bricks and other objects were thrown through the plate-glass windows of a bank, a bookstore, and other businesses. When the windows were replaced, the new ones were promptly smashed until the businesses finally gave up and replaced them with solid masonry and perhaps a small display window.

To protect people and property during the largest demonstrations, it was necessary to call on outside peace officers in addition to the campus patrol and Iowa City police who usually protected the campus. As we gained experience with sheriffs from several counties and state troopers, it was apparent that the troopers were the best disciplined and least likely to aggravate difficult situations by precipitous actions. We were especially pleased with Capt. Lyle Dickinson of the troopers, and felt better when he was in charge. He agreed that his troopers could wear soft hats instead of helmets and leave their firearms in the cars while they walked around campus talking to students.

The protesters wanted to attract as much public attention as possible, and used tactics to maximize their effect. They notified the media in advance of a planned demonstration and willingly responded to questions from reporters. When the reporters and cameras were ready, someone would produce an instant crowd by activating the fire alarms in the residence halls, then leading the residents to the planned site. In a highly publicized case, the planned site was Interstate Highway 80 just north of the city. Hundreds of students blocked all lanes of traffic from both directions. A helicopter with a giant searchlight illuminated the scene, and state troopers directed traffic around the blockade. My administrative colleagues communicated by walkie-talkie radios, but we could only wait for the situation to clear.

In another case, missiles began to land in the major highway intersection at the west end of the Burlington Street bridge over the Iowa River. Bricks and bottles were being lofted from somewhere, but no one could discover the launch site until observers in a helicopter spotted a giant catapult on the roof of a residence hall. Students had constructed it from whole inner tubes and a winch, and it could toss missiles for several hundred feet. We then took steps to tie down some six-foot-diameter concrete sewer pipes waiting to be installed on the hill above the same intersection, to prevent them from being rolled down into the traffic.

The harassing tactics were often more subtle. For example, all of the crystal pendants on the great chandelier in the House Chamber of Old Capitol disappeared mysteriously one night. There was no sign of them for many moons, until workers happened to see a strange box attached to the underside of the large conference table directly under the chandelier. When it was detached, voilà! the truant crystals!

My son Phil was a student senator at that time, and I occasionally saw him in the audience of protesters but noticed that he became annoyed when his colleagues became too abusive. The experience was probably helpful in his later role as judge of the Superior Court in Seattle. Myke was also among the protesters, and I watched from the window of Old Capitol while he, George Forell, a distinguished professor of religion, and 225 others were arrested for refusing to move on as ordered by the police.

The university did not watch helplessly as the disruptions occurred, and many people were arrested and charged with criminal offenses. Leaders then raised bail funds to free them. Students who participated in anti-ROTC demonstrations were charged with violating university regulations, and ordinarily would have been called before the established Committee on Student Conduct. The committee had been disabled, however, when the student government withdrew all of the student members. President Boyd drew upon his lawyer skills to honor due process but not to remain helpless. Rather than trying the cases with a university body lacking students, he called upon Theodore Garfield, retired chief justice of Iowa, to hear the charges and submit his findings to the president. Altogether, Justice Garfield recommended suspension of two students, probation for three others, and probation for SDS (Students for a Democratic Society) as a recognized student organization. Boyd followed all of his recommendations, and appointed a committee of students, faculty, and administrators to conduct a review and recommend a new judicial system.

Students representing a subculture of the protesters demanded that the university provide day care for their children and the children of single mothers in the community. We were sympathetic to the request because they were part of the nontraditional population we were trying to recruit as students. Meeting the request was complicated by restrictions on using university resources for noneducational purposes, but we searched for ways to accommodate the very real need. I appointed an ad hoc advisory committee of faculty members from pediatrics, education, nursing, and sociology to assist us in developing several day care centers located in houses owned by the university. It was not an easy task, because we required the centers to meet all health and safety requirements established by the state, and we also wanted to accommodate a range of cultures, including a counterculture group that was contemptuous of anything that smacked of authority. When they were assigned a house, they adopted the name Free Underground Care Kollective, which produced an acronym expressing their opinion of conventional types, such as the university administrators who provided their facilities. I often wonder how the children from that day care have fared. Before long, faculty and staff members in the university requested child care as an employment benefit, and a well-established system of child care has been developed from its unorthodox beginning.

The general changes in student attitudes during the protest period led to some behavior that was unrelated to civil rights or political issues. The Iowa Memorial Union housed the student-run Bijou Theater, and some of its movies led the university administrators to review our policies on the use of facilities. We refused to censor events, but audiences were restricted to exclude nonstudent juveniles when they showed *Deep Throat* and other rated films. Viewers of one "cult" film followed the lead of patrons nationwide by bringing buckets of spaghetti complete with tomato sauce and splattering it throughout the theater and on the walls. The theater operators were required to pay for the expense of cleaning up after such movies.

My lack of a well-rounded education was exposed by the

"free love" movement and the emergence of gay liberation groups. I agreed that love was greatly preferred to hate as a motivating force, but feared that some of the practices were not "free" and carried a potentially high cost to participants. My advice was not sought, so I could only watch to see what developed and insist that they refrain from behavior that intruded on the privacy of nonparticipants. After all, we were no longer in loco parentis. With reference to the gay and lesbian movement, I wasn't even sure whether homosexuality was defined by what people *were* or by what they *did*. I'm still not sure, but I did know that the people in the movement should be treated with respect and dignity and not deprived of the rights taken for granted by others in the university community. Some of my colleagues announced their homosexuality publicly, but I was not aware of any adverse effect on their professional performance. Rather, lesbians were quite valuable as counselors to students who were uncertain or confused about their sexuality, and helped me to deal with complaints from people at a distance who knew only what they heard secondhand.

The protest activity put an enormous strain on all of the staff in student affairs, and especially on my colleague Phil Jones. He and the staff in the office of campus programs and student activities were in the midst of the planning and turmoil, and were able to exert a moderating influence on some of the more extreme activity as well as to keep us informed about planned demonstrations. Our goal was to protect the right of students to express their opinions, but to keep all activities within the limits of law and university regulations. Dean of Students M. L. Huit was a familiar figure in the midst of demonstrations, and the media carried photographs in which he was holding discussions with demonstrators on the steps of Old Capitol. In 1978, students established the M. L. Huit Faculty Award to "recognize his outstanding dedication and service to students of the University of Iowa during his tenure as Dean of Students." He was later appointed ombudsman, a position he retained until his retirement.

Major crises arose on two occasions. An Administrative Liaison Group (ALG), an ad hoc team of about twenty senior administrators concerned with maintaining security in the face of announced demonstrations, had been established and met as needed. At the height of the destruction and defiance, the group was meeting at a location where we would not be disturbed. Governor Ray was with us because he commanded the National Guard units that were at the ready in the armory, and we were determined not to repeat the tragedy at Kent State University, where the troops killed several student protesters. If the guard was to be ordered into action, the governor wanted the best available information. From that "command post," we were in touch with people equipped with walkie-talkies in the protest crowds. The crisis abated when the crowd activity began to decrease. On another occasion, the protesters, led by the elected student government, tried to force the university to close as an institutional gesture in support of their cause. The entire state was alarmed at the situation, and families were concerned about the safety of their students on campus. We refused to close the university, but gave students who feared for their safety an option: accept their grade at that stage (near the end) of the semester and leave; or complete the semester. Many left, many stayed, but the university continued to operate. I was disappointed to see how many students viewed it as an opportunity to escape final exams even though they did not fear for their safety. Some of those wanted to remain in their student housing units, but had become ineligible to do so when they canceled their registration.

Sometimes it was necessary to break the tension in our grave discussions in the ALG. On one occasion, we were meeting in the president's conference room with the chief of security and the director of student activities to lay security plans for a Woodstock-style rock concert being announced by student leaders who were not really interested in an orderly event. We had decided to remove it to the Macbride field campus about ten miles from town in order to minimize the disturbance to the surrounding community and provide adequate parking for an estimated crowd of 10,000. My longtime friend and assistant to the provost Howard Sokol still remembers our discussion about providing adequate sanitary facilities for a beer-imbibing crowd in a remote location during a concert which might last into the wee-wee hours of the morning. The question was how many portable toilets were needed, and I suggested that we borrow a "well-known" criterion from hydraulic engineering —

the (fictitious) MTBU, or Mean Time Between Urinations. Somehow the tension was relieved. As I always did during controversial events, I went to the field campus on the day of the concert to check on preparations and was confronted by a big burly brute brandishing a bicycle chain who asked, "Are you looking for something, old man?" I admired his pectorals and his perception, because I was surely seeking something — an emergency escape exit.

Protest demonstrations were major news stories throughout the country, and the people of Iowa could not understand why students were rejecting values held dear in their home communities. They inquired, "Are the faculty and staff at the university leading them astray?" The general concern led the media to report on university events thoroughly, and many news stories were generated. To convey the spirit of the time and to avoid viewing my involvement through rose-tinted glasses, I now reproduce some of my comments as reported extensively in the newspapers and university publications.

An interview by Jack Magarrell, reported in the *Des Moines Register*, February 13, 1966, quoted me:

Today's students are more serious than the social aristocrats who dominated American campuses before World War II. Because they are more serious, they resent any restrictions that are not clearly necessary. They want more freedom to control their own affairs and more of a voice in decisions which influence their destinies.

To the extent that they are becoming more responsible and are willing to use this freedom to achieve our educational goals, we are happy to encourage it and cooperate with them.

Regarding student demonstrations on campuses, I said:

I think they are healthy signs. We may not always agree with them but we do believe that they should be concerned. We encourage free expression.

As an educational institution we think we will have failed if we don't develop a critical attitude. Students should not accept everything that is dished out to them. We don't want to dictate what they should or should not do. However, student demonstrations should remain within the law and good taste without interfering with the university's primary purpose of instructing students.

. . . There is a general trend on U.S. campuses toward relaxation of restrictions on students. This can be done and is being done because of the growing maturity of the student population. . . .

Before World War II, college students tended to be members of the social aristocracy, devoting four years to a collegiate fling before settling into the family business that was waiting for them. A few students of less means struggled through college to break into the aristocracy. After World War II and especially after the dawning of the Space Age, the emphasis shifted from family background to individual performance. The large number of students today are under pressure to make good grades, to win scholarships, to prepare themselves for new careers in a fast-changing society. In this race, students have to be more serious.

Dads Day Luncheon Speech (audience of parents and students), November 4, 1967:

A student's ethical standards are pretty well established by the time he or she has reached college age . . . the characteristics which develop during the upper-class years are the result of free choice based upon pre-college moral values.

We must make a clear distinction between the free discussion of deviant behavior and the actual practice thereof. Moral and spiritual matters are taught most effectively by personal example, not by preaching or even by analysis. . . .

The moral values and standards of personal behavior of a university faculty must surely rank near the top if one compares pertinent characteristics among various populations. . . . I am sure that you will find that your children are in solid company. . . .

For students, parents and friends who would understand "why students are like that," remember that these are fine minds applying newly acquired tools of analysis and criticism to the world in which they find themselves. All of us realize that it is not a perfect world, and it is hardly surprising that they find much to criticize. . . .

Although our feelings vary at different times, all of us who have the privilege of working with your sons and daughters are here because we like them, believe in them, and have confidence that they will improve the world if only they are not "turned off" too soon.

My comments were reported in the following item from the *Spectator*, a publication distributed to more than 150,000 alumni, faculty, and friends of the university, November 1970, under the heading "Homegrown Rebels":

> People write angry letters to us at the University, protesting what they see as a very deleterious influence we're having on their progeny. But the students come to us that way.
>
> People who wonder about the undesirable influences their sons and daughters are exposed to don't realize that in many cases we are the ones opposing those influences. The ones who are pushing them are the friends and neighbors of their own kids right there in their hometown.
>
> It's not what we are doing to them, it's what the society in which they're living does to them. They feel they can't express this adequately at home, but when they come here they sure can.

I happened to be the general superintendent of the Sunday school in the First United Methodist Church during the protest era, and had difficulty at the high school level in two ways: finding teachers, and keeping students who were drifting away. Some potential teachers were reluctant to volunteer because they were unsure how to handle students who were disaffected. We did not have a youth pastor at the time, so I agreed to teach the high schoolers after informing the official board that I might not follow an orthodox style. I then operated on the principle that to make rabbit stew you must first get rabbits. I met with the few students who showed up at the first meeting, asked them what aspect of religion they wanted to study, and then found resources to meet that need. When they asked about Catholicism, I took them to mass at the nearby St. Mary's Church. When they asked about Judaism, I introduced them to the rabbi who directed the Hillel Foundation. When they asked about Eastern religions, I invited Robert Baird, who taught the subject in the university, to speak to the class; Professor Baird is now director of the school of religion.

Attendance improved impressively, and as might be expected the questions sometimes strayed from conventional religion. When they asked about the student protests, knowing from the media that I was deeply involved, I asked graduate student Pat Fisher, a leading protester, if she would be willing to meet with the class and speak freely about her rationale. She agreed, and showed up half frozen on a bitter subzero Sunday morning; she had walked a considerable distance to get there. Pat's performance in speaking to the students confirmed my faith and trust in college students. She was frank in criticizing things and people she thought should be criticized, and explained the convictions underlying the protests in a way that was entirely consistent with the principles the church was trying to teach. You can be sure that the grateful teacher drove her back home in a warm car after the class was over.

The general public perceived the protests as endangering the health and safety of people in the university community, and I was often asked whether I feared for my safety in the middle of the angriest demonstrations. My answer was unequivocal: if for some reason I found myself in danger anywhere, I would willingly place my welfare in the hands of the protesters.

We were drawn into the general effort to end apartheid in South Africa because some of the corporations in the university's endowment portfolio had important operations in South Africa. Although university policy makers were sympathetic to the cause, they were placed in a difficult position; the fiduciary responsibility to manage the endowment had been in accordance with principles that did not include social responsibility. The regents finally approved a policy to send university representatives to vote in favor of stockholder resolutions opposing apartheid, and Phil Jones and Casey Mahon duly went to the meetings as designated voters.

The Fine Arts Connection

My involvement in the fine arts arose from the use of space in Iowa Memorial Union, which was part of my responsibility and had the largest auditorium on campus. Events such as symphony concerts and major lectures were staged in its main lounge and the large room also served as a gallery for works of visual art, but change was under way. An expansion of the Art Building and opening the Museum of Art freed up space in the Art Building for new galleries, which were preferred to the main lounge of the Union, and a long-awaited performing arts auditorium and new music building became a reality when the regents gave final approval to the plans.

With strong support from Darrell Wyrick, director (later president) of the University of Iowa Foundation, the Iowa Center for the Arts was created in 1968 with the mission to coordinate and support public events produced by the fine arts departments and related administrative units. Because of my responsibility for the Union and eventually for Hancher Auditorium, I was designated to chair the center. The board met monthly to exchange information, minimize scheduling conflicts, plan cooperative programs, and determine the needs for special resources. In addition, we wanted to utilize the exceptional communication potential of the fine arts to take full advantage of the increasing diversity in the campus community. I defined its mission with the following statement:

> From the time of its establishment, the University of Iowa has incorporated the fine arts into its institutional mission of teaching, creative scholarship, and outreach to the people of Iowa. Curricula in the literary, visual, and performing arts, and public exhibits, lectures, readings, plays, opera, films, dance and musical concerts for students and others in the local and state communities have naturally led to identification of the University as a center for the creative and performing arts.

In recent years, the Voxman Music Building, the Museum of Art, and Hancher Auditorium have been erected on the west bank of the Iowa River (the campus "mall") where the School of Art and Art History and the university theater were also located, according to a plan to bring the arts together. Because it is devoted to the needs of those who are concerned with the fine arts and serves as physical evidence of the university's dedication, this portion of the campus has been designated the Iowa Center for the Arts. The arts are much more than a collection of landscaped buildings, of course, and the concept of the center includes all those whose efforts are dedicated to advancing the arts, wherever they and their works might be located on campus. At the present time, the creative writing, film, and dance programs are housed on the east campus, but they are considered important conceptual components of the center. To further quote from my mission statement:

> Formal recognition of the concept of a Center and the designation of a site are not only acknowledgment of a desirable circumstance, but are also an expression of the University's conviction that the collective influence of the several arts can be much more that the sum of their individual effects. Activities of the Center are planned and directed to contribute to the cultural life of Iowa and this region of the United States, recognizing that the academic programs report through their appropriate college channels to the Dean of Faculties. The academic departments and the public areas

(Museum of Art and Hancher Auditorium) therefore work in coordination to achieve maximum benefit for the constituencies both inside and outside the University.

The original departments and representatives in the center were: Department of Art and Art History, Professor Frank Seiberling; Center for the Book, Professor K. K. Merker; Writers' Workshop, Professor John Leggett; Dance, Professor Judith Allen; Hancher Auditorium, James Wockenfuss; Museum of Art, Ulfert Wilkie; Music, Professor Himie Voxman; Theater Arts, Lewin Goff; Darrel Wyrick, president, University of Iowa Foundation; and English professor John Gerber, consultant. As we gained experience with the new arrangement, we added Mary Louise Plautz as arts outreach educator.

Creation of the center was closely related to the anticipated opening of Hancher Auditorium in 1972. The long-awaited dream of the performing arts departments and Pres. Virgil M. Hancher was to be our principal showcase for the performing arts, just as the Museum of Art is our public showcase for the visual arts. Careful plans had been made to provide financial support for the auditorium, such as management staff, custodial staff and supplies, security, general expense, and utilities. Revenue bonds were sold to support capital expenses, to be retired by income from a dedicated student fee. Program expenses were to be supported from box office income, grants, and gifts. Managing the auditorium and keeping harmony among capable managers with artistic temperaments required a special talent, and James Wockenfuss met the bill for many years. He had been hired while the building was still under construction, and detected some planning flaws such as a heavy beam so low that completed scenery could not be moved intact from the scene shop to the stage. All went reasonably well, and the building was completed with alterations. He established an effective working partnership with the Joffrey Dance Company with strong support from Professor Lewis January, and sponsored summer residencies that helped promote dance as a fine art, not just a form of skilled physical exercise. After many years, the program in dance was elevated to a department in the College of Liberal Arts, offering bachelor's and master's degrees. He obtained grants to subsidize programs that had high educational value but could not support their cost at the box office, as well as performances by young artists who had not yet established a reputation. Some of his choices went on to achieve worldwide acclaim, such as Van Cliburn.

We wanted the auditorium to be a major educational asset and encouraged students to attend events by offering reduced ticket prices, group discounts, and the opportunity to order tickets at an early date. Because of our experience with student-sponsored concerts in the Fieldhouse, we were worried that they might want to use the new auditorium for rock concerts. Fortunately, students preferred the much larger Carver Hawkeye Arena, using the auditorium only for quieter events. Students' behavior at Hancher Auditorium surprised and pleased us, because they appreciated the beautiful setting and did not leave the indescribable litter that had been characteristic of rock concerts in the Fieldhouse. The reference to rock concerts reminds me that I attended them in connection with my supervisory responsibility, and may have suffered permanent loss of hearing, even though I wore earplugs and watched from a room at the back of the building. The sound level seemed to be higher than that of the machine guns I fired in the army.

Although we were prepared to support the direct cost of operating the new auditorium, the performing arts departments soon found that their long-awaited dream placed an impossible burden on their academic resources. Its huge stage was ideal for symphony, musical theater, and opera productions, but demanded technical support and supplies for which the departments of theatre, music, and dance were not prepared. Resentment increased when the original directors retired and were replaced by directors who had not experienced the realization of a dream. They were especially critical of the high rent charged for use of the auditorium, even though it was much less than what outside users paid.

When Wockenfuss retired to head the new performing arts center at the University of California at Davis, I appointed a search committee chaired by Professor John Gerber, a highly regarded Mark Twain scholar who had retired after a distinguished tenure as head of the Department of English. A national search identified a prime candidate in our own Department of Theatre in the person of Wallace Chappell, who was appointed. His knowledge of the performing arts and his personality enabled him to maintain the operation of the auditorium at a high level, with events from many cultures and parts of the world. His desire to use the performing arts as an educational asset was in close harmony with the university's emphasis on increasing interaction among the various ethnic groups on campus, as well as exposing students to talent from the Pacific nations as well as Europe. Chappell and I worked together very well, and I was able to solve some of the problems that had led to the departure of Wockenfuss by allocating additional funds to relieve the strain on the budgets of music, theatre, and dance.

The auditorium has continued to forge ahead under his expert direction. He brings artists from around the world and young artists who have not yet achieved a strong reputation. His excellent management has attracted numerous grants to underwrite events with high educational value but the inability to support their cost through the box office alone. Artists like to perform in the auditorium because of the well-trained staff, gracious accommodation of their needs, and enthusiastic audiences. Through the creative leadership of Wockenfuss and Chappell, Hancher Auditorium has realized the university's hope of a regional jewel for presenting the performing arts.

In keeping with general university policy at the time, I shifted many of the other programs under my supervision from the general fund to user fees. This freed up funds for reallocation to meet some of the needs of the academic departments. In this way, I funded an opera production unit for music and dance, a stage manager and assistantships for theater, an education outreach coordinator, scholarships for talented freshman prospects for the symphony orchestra, and rent for academic events in the auditorium, for example. For good measure, I also provided assistantships for the Department of Art and Art History and a copy machine for the Iowa Writers' Workshop because our goals included improving the academic quality of all fine arts departments. To avoid loss of the reallocated funds to the distinctly different priorities of the academic departments during the inevitable hard times ahead, I kept them in my general budget.

Working with administrators in the fine arts was different from my work with student service directors because they needed more flexibility to manage resources, and some of them reported primarily to the dean of liberal arts. I tried to keep the dean informed of my actions, but as noted above, kept allocations under my control because I knew that the dean and I had understandably different priorities. My inexperience in the fine arts did not seem to be a problem because I was fully aware of the deficiency and did not make a pretense of understanding artistic matters. One potential difficulty was averted when Sam Becker was appointed acting chair of the Department of Theatre for a year. His quiet manner and long familiarity with the university (he and I both enrolled as freshmen in 1940) equipped him admirably to assist the university with special problems from time to time. He did this so well that many faculty and administrators encouraged him to accept the position of chief administrative officer when there was a vacancy.

Differing opinions on nudity in artistic events caused us to develop a policy on the matter following a performance of *Hair* by the Pilobolus Dance Company. I had relied on the judgment of the faculty in the relevant area in matters related to sex, and did not have any objection to artistic exposure of the human body. Some people criticized the university for presenting an event in which some of the dancers were nude, and demanded that we exclude such performances. Censorship is inconsistent with the concept of a university as a place where ideas can be expressed freely in search of the truth, and the faculty in relevant areas are the best judges of artistic value. We did not retreat from our position, but were careful that the advertisements for events informed the public that a performance might not be appropriate for children, or that it had "adult content."

In 1970, my title was changed to vice provost, and in 1972 to vice president for student services and dean of academic affairs. Boyd had been appointed president in 1969, and with the new title I was still reporting to him with responsibility for establishing and managing all of the budgets as well as hiring and evaluating the performance of the student service directors. My administrative years coincided with a period of rapidly increasing enrollment, and the financial resources followed suit.

We also wanted to use the exceptional communication potential of the fine arts to support another major university priority: incorporating the increasing diversity of the community into the fabric of the university's total operation. I expressed that idea in this excerpt from *New Dawns*:

Fine arts are especially valuable in promoting inter-cultural understanding because they are universal media of communication, transcending boundaries of time, distance, economics, and the barriers created in the tactical struggles for dominance by exaggerating ethnic and gender differences. Paupers and princesses can be similarly enthralled at a musical or dance performance, a play can illuminate principles and relationships which defy purely verbal communication, and the visual arts can please or repel individuals without reference to race and gender. A special emphasis on the fine arts is therefore recommended not only for their great value in the cultural development of the individual, but also as powerful allies in promoting understanding and appreciation among the diverse members of the community. The active participants, some of whom may not be members of the social elite, may also improve their self-esteem and advance their careers through the public opportunity to demonstrate their personal and group talents.

The faculty and administrators responsible for the fine arts at the University of Iowa are keenly aware of these values, and have made exemplary use of the rich resources at their disposal. When Voxman Music Building and Hancher Auditorium were constructed along the west bank of the Iowa River in 1972, they joined the Museum of Art, the Department of Art and Art History and University Theater to complete a plan created earlier by President Virgil Hancher. I joined other university administrators, the directors of the fine arts departments, and Darrell Wyrick, Director of the University of Iowa Foundation, in creating the Iowa Center for the Arts to increase the effectiveness of the fine arts by providing coordination and financial support. One important step was the appointment of arts educators in the Center with the specific responsibility to improve the arts appreciation of the general public and supplement the programs offered by the public schools. Mary Louise Plautz, is especially well known for her skill in working with faculty to produce special performances for children, and Hancher Auditorium has often been filled with elementary school children from eastern Iowa who arrive in their own buses, accompanied by teachers.

I wrote the following statement in April 1975, after Hancher Auditorium opened; it indicates the way in which the university has proceeded to extend the influence of the arts.

With reference to incorporating ethnic diversity into the institutional fabric, the schools of art, music, and theater were among the leading academic units preparing teachers and administrators for the Historically Black Colleges and universities discussed earlier in this document [*New Dawns*], and that contribution is acknowledged. Equally important has been their use of performances and exhibits on campus to underscore the deep reservoir of talent among the diverse populations of the world and within the university community. The Department of Dance has joined their ranks more recently, and the Museum of Art and Hancher Auditorium have extended the influence of the arts to a wider audience in this region. Artists are now attracted from throughout the world to supplement the core of events which represent the university's unique contribution, using its own students and faculty.

My working definition of "diversity" was quite broad: students should come from all geographic areas, from both low-income and affluent families, various religions, and from the many ethnic groups in the world community. As a state university, it is expected that all qualified Iowans would be admitted, although the enrollment in some programs is limited by our capacity to provide a quality education. Faculty and administrators should include representatives of the diverse components of the American population as a whole, on the assumption that the educational process includes interactions outside the classrooms — living areas, athletic and intramural programs, recreational facilities, and public aspects of the fine arts programs — as well as in formal courses.

"Culture" refers to the customary beliefs, social forms, and material traits of a racial, religious, or social group, and it is assumed that those qualities can best be understood and appreciated by creating a total environment that encourages intellectual interchange, not the mere coexistence of diverse groups. I encouraged and supported many groups and activities that contributed to such an understanding, including visual and performing arts, intramural sports, extracurricular lectures, and travel abroad. Special attention was given to groups that students were willing to sponsor on their own volition, such as the Voices of Soul gospel choir, the Baleadores Zapatistas, the Old Gold Singers, the Native American Dance Troupe, the Scottish Highlanders, and the Black Action Theater. My support consisted of providing space and instructors, and money for publicity, equipment, and space rental. The programs served the dual purpose of developing the participants' talents while enabling them to inform the academic community about the cultures they represented. As the student population became more diverse, each group contributed to the campus traditions, but not in an exclusive manner. For example, the Scottish Highlanders are committed to Scottish piping, drumming, and dancing, but the membership has included students of many ancestries, including American minorities. Similarly, the Voices of Soul gospel choir started as an all-black group in 1968, but nearly half of the members of later choirs were of European ancestry or other American minorities who enjoy singing and playing gospel music.

Human Rights, Diversity, and Excellence

In the course of my lifetime, the world has evolved at a dizzy pace, marked by a deep economic depression, an atrociously ugly war, and an unprecedented expansion of technology. No one has escaped the effects of those events, and I have been directly involved in them first as an almost helpless participant and then in a progressively active role.

Down through the ages, large wars have led to substantial alterations in the evolution of societies. Scientific and technical efforts directed toward the development of weapons have produced not only deadlier weapons, but also devices that revolutionize the way that people live. The borders that define societies have been altered irreversibly, and dominant cultures have grown into dynasties. Repulsive as it was, World War II left a legacy of scientific and technological development that has transformed and improved the ways that people live and communicate. The legacy also has a more human face — Americans began to ask why we could cooperate so effectively to resist an external enemy yet revert to the racist and sexist antagonisms that prevent the full enjoyment of the pleasures of peace and foment internal stress. Our attempts to deal with this dilemma have led to decisions by the courts and actions by Congress and presidents that loosened the shackles of oppressed minorities.

I view the period since World War II as the era of human rights in America and at the University of Iowa. My principal involvement in the era has been through my association with the university, so I will focus on the university experience as a microcosm of the larger society. During my half century as student, professor, and dean, five men served as its president. My administrative responsibilities began with an appointment by Howard Bowen, but an important committee appointment by Virgil Hancher turned out to be the first step in a change of career. From that perspective, I present a brief review of the evolution of human rights in the university as influenced by those presidents, and the effect of our policies on educational quality. I have always viewed the president as the center, not the top, of the executive structure in a community of scholars, so that the method of selecting a president may provide insight into the way that faculty, students, and staff are brought into the community.

The appointment of Virgil M. Hancher coincided with my enrollment as a freshman in 1940. He had an excellent record as an undergraduate at the university, graduated from the law school, and was practicing law in Chicago. He had no experience in teaching or educational administration, and the circumstances of his selection illustrate the style for filling vacancies before the era of human rights and affirmative action. As recounted by Stow Persons in *The University of Iowa in the Twentieth Century: An Institutional History*:

> Previously the governing board had chosen its presidents from within the academic community, acting on the implicit assumption that appropriate candidates were to be found among those already experienced in teaching and educational administration. Upon the retirement of President Gilmore the initial impulse of the board was to turn again to the academics, and it is likely that a traditional type of appointment would have been made but for the fact that a deadlock developed between the principal on-campus candidates: Paul Packer, Dean of Education, and the graduate dean, George Stoddard. Fearing that the choice of either

man would entail a legacy of bitterness, the board sought someone not identified with local factions. At that moment Regent W. Earl Hall, an energetic board member long active in alumni affairs, vigorously promoted the candidacy of his classmate Virgil M. Hancher.

As might be expected from that beginning, President Hancher was a competent administrator but not an educational leader. In the final analysis, academic quality is determined by the performance of the faculty, and he left their selection to strong department heads with final approval in the hands of Provost Harvey Davis. The "old boy" network for filling faculty and administrative vacancies had led to few women and very few ethnic minorities at the time of his retirement. Regarding human rights in general, Hancher saw no need for change until his final years as president. As described earlier, minority students were admitted without any general university policy regarding discrimination, and thus they were at the mercy of individual staff members in seeking access to university facilities and employment. African American students were finally permitted to live in university housing after World War II, when the maturity of returning veterans changed the attitudes of the student body. That evolutionary change serves to illustrate the conservative style of administration before the era of human rights.

As far as I am aware, Hancher accepted my appointment as the first African American professor in the history of the university as consistent with his concept of faculty. My appointment represented a triumph of merit over tradition owing to an exceptionally strong recommendation from Howe, the department head. In his history, Persons stated: ". . . in addition to scholarly accomplishment and teaching ability he [Hancher] believed that prospective faculty appointees should be of acceptable nationality, religion, marital status, and other 'more intimate personal details.'" With that perspective, it is unlikely that he would have foreseen the substantial changes that grew from his appointment of a Committee on Human Rights in the penultimate year of his tenure.

One obvious effect of the emphasis on human rights is the ethnic and gender makeup of the community of students, faculty, and staff. Although minority students were the least privileged from the university's beginning and through the Hancher years, students in general and undergraduates in particular were denied much of the freedom taken for granted by their contemporaries in the nonacademic world, under the guise of a doctrine of in loco parentis, Women students fared worse than their male counterparts under the doctrine, but they suffered even more from the stereotypes limiting their participation in the full range of university programs. As in the case of ethnic minorities, persons with physical disabilities were obliged to cope with a system that made few provisions for their needs. This brief description might be considered the baseline from which to measure changes during the era of human rights.

Bowen was a contrast to Hancher in several ways: he had a stellar record of teaching and administration, and instead of laissez faire, his aggressive promotion of academic excellence rejuvenated some of the faculty and annoyed others. He addressed the neglect of minority recruitment by establishing the Educational Opportunity program and a related scholarship fund to assist low-income minority students. Not needing the prod of a policy on affirmative action that was developed later, he selected me to join his team of human rights activists. His policies led to the elimination of the in loco parentis posture toward students, and he encouraged the enrollment of women in the professional colleges.

Willard Boyd accelerated the pace of human rights reform by recruiting ethnic minorities in the student body and on the faculty and staff. Affirmative action at all levels became a hallmark of his administration, and he set a precedent by inviting Iowa alumna May Brodbeck from the University of Minnesota to become the first woman to hold the position vice president for academic affairs. He then gave full support toward creation of the Council on the Status of Women, took steps to measure and remedy the inequity between salaries for men and women, and gave credit for unpaid volunteer service by applicants for employment. His reform of the university committees redefined the role of committees in university governance, making them advisory to the administration. Administrators were accordingly removed from all general committees, with a balance of faculty, student, and staff members, gender balance, and minority representation in the membership and in the chairs. Accessibility for persons with disabilities was greatly improved by his program to remove physical and attitudinal barriers to their full participation in all phases of university activity.

In contrast to the "old boy network" of the past, a policy of affirmative action now controls the selection, appointment, and promotion of all university employees, and students are treated as adults responsible for their actions. Today's university includes substantial numbers of people from populations that were neglected or effectively excluded fifty years ago. Women, minorities, and people with physical disabilities are included in all phases of university operation, with assistance to help them overcome the effects of past discrimination.

James Freedman gave full support to the reforms initiated by Bowen and Boyd, and encouraged the identification and training of women for administrative responsibility. His emphasis on private fund-raising expanded resources for implementing goals of diversity and quality. Programs to improve undergraduate education included special attention to minority students and those in the fine arts. The Covenant with Quality and the associated Iowa Endowment 2000 were noted for an emphasis on raising funds for human resources — faculty, students, and staff, without any component for bricks and mortar — and their fund-raising success provided resources to support development of a diverse community.

Hunter Rawlings emphasized strategic planning with the goal to improve Iowa's ranking among universities in the twenty-first century. His plan, "Achieving Distinction: Strategic Planning for the University of Iowa," set goals for excellence of undergraduate, graduate and professional programs, faculty distinction, and ties to our external constituency. A specific major goal embraced "An academic community diverse in gender, race, ethnicity, and nationality. . . . The opportunity to work and study in a diverse community helps prepare students for life in a multicultural, multiethnic, and multiracial national and international society. We also recognize our obligation to extend educational opportunities to previously excluded groups."

Mary Sue Coleman succeeded Rawlings in 1995, and I view

her as the star exhibit in a case for human rights policies and associated procedures. She is a superb president by all measures; having continued the major emphasis on excellence, she continues to broaden the diversity of the university community. Coleman has assembled an excellent team of central administrators to lead the university into the twenty-first century, and is a splendid example and ambassador to our alumni and to the people of Iowa. Chalk up another triumph of merit over tradition.

The university's search for excellence during the last third of the twentieth century has yielded encouraging progress in educational quality by all traditional measures — peer evaluations, student scores on standardized tests, faculty production, private fund-raising, and competition for contracts and grants. Its quality has also been enhanced on a measure appropriate to the era: the greatly increased diversity of the total community constitutes a superior learning environment because it is more representative of the society in which the students will spend the rest of their lives. I see the parallel emergence of excellence and an emphasis on human rights, not as coincidental developments, but as cause and effect in freeing the university to use the human resources of society more effectively. It has thereby achieved academic excellence, not because the previously excluded populations are collectively superior, but because merit is taking precedence over prejudice and tradition.

I cannot and probably should not resist the temptation to make a personal statement at this point in the story. Although the national emphasis on civil and human rights followed my entry into the life of the university, I benefited from the underlying concern for the plight of citizens who were suppressed by traditional social and political prejudices. It has been my privilege to assist many others in arousing the conscience of the people and guiding their energy into an era of goodwill and human rights. The "many others" and their actions have been identified herein, and I am one of an uncountable number of citizens who are indebted to them.

IV

The Free Years

Retirement

All my life, I have been having the time of my life, but I finally passed the professional baton to others. After eighteen months of working half time as part of the university's phased retirement program, I retired fully in 1991 but retained my office and the services of Sherilyn Sorge, my excellent secretary. I continued to serve on search committees for positions such as vice president for research, director of the University of Iowa Hospitals and Clinics, and faculty for my academic department. The new dean of engineering, Richard Miller, appointed me to chair a diversity advisory committee for the college, a task I accepted with relish because it was essentially a continuation of my active service. I wrote a paper for the International Conference, "Numerical Ship Hydrodynamics," that honored my esteemed colleague Louis Landweber, and continue to attend faculty meetings in the department of mechanical engineering. Other activities included being a member and secretary for the Board of Fellows of the school of religion and attending staff meetings for Opportunity at Iowa, the Iowa Institute of Hydraulic Research, and the staff of the vice president for academic affairs. At the request of Robert Morris, grandson of longtime publisher J. B. Morris, I wrote an article, "The History of African Americans at the University," for a special centennial edition of the *Iowa Bystander*, a Des Moines newspaper serving African Americans in Iowa. One of my more substantial efforts was to develop the program proposal for the Institute for Learning and Development I will describe in a chapter on unrealized dreams. In 1995, I was appointed to the steering committee for the university's sesquicentennial celebration, and for that occasion wrote the book *New Dawns: A 150-year Look at Human Rights at the University of Iowa*.

From time to time, I had spoken at the annual Martin Luther King ceremonies, and continued to do so during retirement. Pres. Mary Sue Coleman gave a very gracious introduction when I gave the speech in 1997; she has been a strong advocate for human rights as well as for excellence in all aspects of the university's operation.

The tragic fate of an esteemed colleague left me with wounds that will never heal: my search for a director of the evaluation and examination service in 1973 led us to T. Anne Cleary, who had been vice president of the College Board in New York, a national testing agency. She was superbly qualified for the position we sought to fill, and served with distinction. She was quite close to her brother Paul, and referred to his daughter as the perfect baby. Her widowed father moved to Iowa City, and she was pleased that he was quite popular with the women in the nursing home where he lived, escorting them to concerts and otherwise being chivalrous. She was dismayed when her father contracted Alzheimer's disease, and I saw at firsthand the agony of a strong and independent woman watching helplessly while a loved one drifted away. When she suffered a serious illness, I visited her in the hospital and rejoiced at her recovery.

When a position of associate vice president for academic affairs was created, I recommended her for the job and she was appointed. The duties in her new job included serving as the university's designee for final appeal in student academic complaints before they were sent to the regents. A doctoral student who was outraged by his failure to receive a distinguished award bought handguns, practiced at a firing range, and on November 1, 1991, he killed his rival for the award and three professors who were involved in the selection, then proceeded to Cleary's office. She was in conference, but he demanded that her secretary call her out. He then placed a gun to her head and fired. For good measure, he shot and permanently paralyzed the secretary, went down the hall past my office, and shot himself in a small library at the other end of the building. A plaza north of Old Capitol was named in memory of Dr. T. Anne Cleary, but it has not relieved my sorrow at losing a colleague I brought to the university.

For three years beginning in fall 1990, I combined my interests in religion and music by singing in the choir of the First United Methodist Church, which I had joined as a freshman. Since retiring I have maintained a reasonably busy schedule. Beginning in 1991, I served a six-year term as trustee of the Iowa City Public Library, and I am serving my second three-year appointment to the Board of Trustees of the University of Iowa Foundation. From time to time, I have been invited by teachers to read my favorite stories, such as Theseus and the Minotaur, to third- and fourth-grade children in the Iowa City schools, or to tell the children in Helen Lemme School about the woman for whom their school was named, since I knew her personally for many years. When Breakthrough, Inc. was created in 1994 to market a computer-based curriculum to teach children to read, I was elected to the board of directors and served until the company was sold to a publishing company in 1997.

After Wynonna's death, the children often included me in their vacation plans. In December 1991, Richard, his wife Alaka, and their children Shanti and Eric accompanied Alaka's parents to India, and invited me to go along. While Alaka's father Kamishwar Wali attended a professional meeting in Bombay, the rest of us proceeded to Ujjain, the city where Alaka and her mother Kashi had been born, and I became acquainted with four generations of the Wali family.

Richard and I then took a side trip to Nepal for three days to explore the area around Kathmandu and flew via Nepal Airline to view Mount Everest and the nearby mountains. (I recalled that in 1973 Christine and her husband James Walters had hiked for several weeks through the Himalayas of Nepal and Sikkim, the location of his Peace Corps days.) We visited the very interesting National Museum and the Museum of Natural History before climbing to the Monkey Temple (Swayambhuna-tath) on a tall (for my arthritic legs) mountain. On every hand, there was evidence of the cheapness of human labor. Taxis had not only a driver, but a second man who served as guide. Our travel agent sent a man to the airport at six A.M. to stand in line for the best tickets on a flight to view Mount Everest (Sagarmatha); there are usually more staff than customers in restaurants, hotel lobbies, and shops. Tiny shops had two or three staff with no customers for hours at a time. We bought Thangka paintings, produced at an atelier near the royal palace by skilled craftsmen under the watchful eye of a monk, and sold at a tiny shop staffed by very well-informed salesmen.

With labor so cheap, there was evidence of poverty everywhere. A small city of temporary shanties filled the Bagmati River Valley, far below the surface of a destructive flood the previous year. Traffic moved across a temporary embankment because the flood had destroyed the main bridge. We visited a Buddhist monastery that was preparing for the arrival of a new family, and viewed a crematory platform on the banks of a tributary of the Ganges.

After we rejoined the others in Delhi, they hired a car and driver and the seven of us revisited some of places that Wynonna and I had seen in 1976. In Bombay and in Poona, we met several of Kamishwar's family so that Shanti and Eric were able to establish a firsthand bond with forebears, aunts, uncles, and cousins on both sides of the family.

In July 1992, I joined other members of the University of Iowa President's Club on a tour of several cities in France, a cruise on the Rhône River, and a ride on the Très Gran Vitesse train from Mâcon to Paris.

In December 1992, a memorable family reunion was held in Grand Cayman, British West Indies. I enjoyed a week in the Caribbean sunshine with Philip, his wife Susan, and their children Anthony and Monica; Christine and her son Matthew (Jim's mother had died a few weeks earlier, and he remained at home); Michael, his wife Carol Torres, and their children Peter and Sarah; Richard, his wife Alaka Wali, and their children Shanti and Eric; and Peter, his wife Mary, and their children Robert, Neil, and Katherine. We stayed in four furnished condominiums, and each family prepared one evening meal for the entire group. My contribution was a final dinner at the Wharf restaurant overlooking the Caribbean. Activities included swimming, snorkeling, scuba diving lessons, a ride in a submarine, and other activities using the areas near Seven Mile Beach. Time-share options for the last week in December were purchased for two of the condominiums, and they were used by members of the family and guests in 1994 and 1996.

In the summer of 1993, Peter, Mary, Robert, Neil, Katherine, and I traveled by AMTRAK to visit Richard and his family in Westfield, New Jersey, with a side trip to Niagara Falls. Later in the summer, I joined Philip, Susan, Anthony, and Monica and Susan's mother, Rose Bale, on a cruise to Alaska through the Inland Passage.

In summer 1994, I tagged along with Michael and Richard and their families and guests David, Susan, and Benjamin Snyder for a vacation near Kitty Hawk on the Outer Banks of North Carolina. Two years later, I joined Michael, Carol, Peter, and Sarah for a week of maritime pleasures on Emerald Isle, another of the Outer Banks. In August 1997, I was again the guest of Rick and Alaka for another vacation with their family and the Snyders on Hatteras Island.

In January and February 1997, Richard and I joined a tour of ten people, including Susan and Sandy Boyd, to the Republic of South Africa under the sponsorship of the Field Museum in Chicago. We visited historic sites around Johannesburg and Pretoria, and took the famous Blue Train from Pretoria to Cape Town. All accommodations were first class, and the gourmet meals included entrées of impala, wildebeest, and ostrich steak. We visited the prison on Robben Island where Nelson Mandela spent eighteen of his twenty-seven years in prisons, explored the Cape area and wine country, and spent four days viewing the magnificent flora and fauna of Kruger National Park (we were restricted to the inside of vans; the park belongs to the wild).

Life in an apartment was acceptable with regard to the chores of housekeeping, laundry, shopping, and cooking, but living alone for the first time in my life was hardly tolerable. So in 1994, I moved from the apartment that Wynonna and I had occupied from 1988 until her death, and moved to Walden Place, a retirement residence with 100 apartments accommodating individuals or couples; the average age is eighty-five. When I moved, I donated most of my household furnishings to the Wesley Foundation, Goodwill Industries, the loan bank for foreign students, and the Domestic Violence Intervention Program (DVI). Boxes of books were given to the Iowa City Public Library and the Women's Resource and Action Center. When people arrived to carry articles to DVI, I was surprised and pleased to see that they were Volunteers in Service to America.

At Walden Place, three meals are served daily, giving us a chance to meet one another. Seating is first come, first served, and the earliest arrivals are in place one hour or more before mealtime. Following a lifelong habit in keeping appointments, I am seldom late, but never more than three minutes early, so that almost everyone else is in place by the time I arrive. That gives me the opportunity to select any table that has an empty seat, and I have dined with most of the residents at one time or another. They come from a surprisingly wide area, from Washington to Cuba, New England to California. Most of those from out of state have sons, daughters, nieces, or nephews who work in Iowa City, including the very large university hospital.

The most senior of the residents at Walden Place is Carrie Hackmann, who was born in 1899 and is one of the most interesting dinner companions. Although she is legally blind, Carrie is quite lively and keeps in contact with events better than most of us. Each morning, Carrie is joined in her apartment by a small group for devotions, and a favorite pastime is listening to talking books provided by the Commission for the Blind. Through her I have enjoyed hearing of a solo trip to the North Pole (almost), how guide dogs for the blind are selected and trained, and current books on English history and living conditions in New York City. Two of her all-time favorites are *How Green Was My Valley* by Llewellyn, and *The Doll Maker*.

Constance (not her real name) came to live at Walden Place the year after I did, and soon attracted the attention of the other residents because of her disorientation. I was offended by the thoughtless and unkind remarks directed at her by a handful of residents, and occasionally helped her to find a place in the dining room or return to her apartment. To my surprise, she began to ask for me when she needed help, and we became very good friends. I met her three children and some of her very talented grandchildren. We attended movies, the opera, and church, and made many trips to area parks. When she eventually moved to a nursing home in another town, a fate that she dreaded, I visited her regularly because she had pleaded with me not to abandon her. By then, she had become such a dear friend that I happily continued to make the forty-nine-mile round trip more than 100 times during the first year, and for another year I often joined her for the Sunday worship service at the nursing home.

While living at Walden Place I continue to serve on a few boards and committees, played the role of Hoke Coleburn in *Driving Miss Daisy*, directed by Janey Yates at the Johnson County Senior Center, and joined other men in the Walden Warblers, which began as a barbershop "quartet," but is now generously endowed with eight voices (perhaps it requires eight elderly voices to make as much noise as four usually do). When we decided to present a program of Irish music on St. Patrick's Day, I suggested that it include *Danny Boy*, which I had first played as a solo on the baritone horn and later sang to entertain our children. To my dismay, some of the group demurred because they were not familiar with it, and suggested that I sing while they hummed. I thus found that I had suddenly become a soloist.

Although my job has been to attract students to the university, I have not lost sight of the larger goal of extending to prospective students the opportunity to attend the institution best suited to their needs. That may mean a smaller institution, one with a religious affiliation, or one with a history of serving an ethnic minority population. I worked to assure that the university prepares all students for success in our society, but motivation is such a critical factor that some students are most likely to survive the college experience by attending a different college. For that reason, I continue to assist the specialized institutions by contributing to their scholarship funds. I found that Davenport has the most ethnically diverse population in Iowa and St. Ambrose University serves its community very well, so I continue to support its work. In addition, I contribute to the United Negro College Fund and the American Indian College Fund, which provide opportunity to students who prefer a special educational environment.

Among my most prized mementos are gifts from student organizations in appreciation for my efforts on their behalf: plaques from the Black Law Students Association and the Black Student Union; a red shawl and a Navajo vase from the American Indian Student Association; a beautiful case from the Council on the Status of Latinos that contains miniatures hand-crafted by Dolores Duran-Cerda; a clock from the Student National Medical Association; a videotape of a concert by the Voices of Soul, dedicated to Wynonna; a Brotherhood Award established by the Interfraternity Council, awarded to a student each year; a Leadership Award established by the Riverfest Council, also awarded to a student each year; a sweatshirt from the Society of Women Engineers; a tribute from the Scottish Highlanders in their newsletter for winter 1989. The Philip G. Hubbard Human Rights Award was created by the University Committee on Human Rights in 1981, and is awarded each year to a student who has made the most outstanding contribution to human rights.

I was awarded the Hancher-Finkbine Medallion for Leadership, Learning and Loyalty in 1993 and was designated a University of Iowa Distinguished Alumnus in 1994 by the Alumni Association. In 1996, I was selected in the charter group for membership in the University of Iowa College of Engineering Distinguished Alumni Academy. After I retired in 1991, my friends and colleagues in the university arranged a dinner party that filled the IMU ballroom, invited all of my children, and showered me with gifts. One honor will be remembered long after I have disappeared — a plot of land between the Iowa River and Old Capitol was named "Hubbard Park." When people see the prominent native limestone slab and wonder "Who was Hubbard?" perhaps they will find the answer in this book. To my great pleasure, the park is across Iowa Avenue from the Becker Communications Building, named for my longtime friend Sam Becker.

My colleagues in the College of Engineering warmed my heart and reassured me that I had not gone too far "astray" by arranging a reception and presenting me with a formal proclamation detailing my academic and professional record, and bestowing me with the title Emeritus Professor of Mechanical Engineering.

The people in the university and in Iowa City have been very kind to our family, and my gratitude for their generosity cannot be expressed adequately; as we used to say in our family and in our church, I can only "pass it on."

Dreams

What is a life story? Is it sufficient to recount details, tell of accomplishments and failures, joys and sorrows, guardians and giants, and leave to others the task of deciding what it means? Some readers will try, and I may be able to help. So far, I have described my preparation for life, the passage from an original family to the nurture of a new generation, and a professional career. Has it all converged to what might be described as a mission? We have seen that my journey was not planned, but neither was it a random wandering. What was the underlying influence, however subtle, that guided my trip through an uncharted territory of challenge and opportunity?

I have referred to a wise mother, a supportive family, a philosophy underlain by religious belief, and a pragmatic approach to the real world. To the extent that I have had a mission, it has been defined by a concern for the welfare of humankind individually and collectively, and a passion to make a difference by direct action and by teaching. With adequate but not complete success, I aimed to excel in each primary undertaking, and expected only that success would lead to opportunity, not to a reward. Opportunities would appear, not by divine providence, but because people of goodwill with a mission could advance their goals by developing and using my talents. My challenge was to consider various desirable alternatives and select the ones that were compatible with my guiding philosophy, with the times, and with the needs of those who depended on me. Entrepreneurial enterprises were not ruled out; in fact, I created and successfully operated two companies, but chose a more Spartan scholarly life.

Although I did not adopt a long-range goal or have a dream at an early age, I developed goals as my career developed. Many of the dreams have been realized, as told in my story thus far. Is there a major unrealized dream? The answer is yes.

As my career developed and I learned more about the reasons for some characteristics of our society that disturbed me, I began to dream of ways to help. My work as an engineer and academic administrator featured problem solving, and I have never been satisfied merely to identify a problem and leave it for someone else to solve. One of my major concerns has been the presence of poverty in the midst of an affluent society, and in keeping with my experience, I viewed education as an ideal way to elevate the people near the bottom of the economic ladder. The Educational Opportunity program was an important step in implementing that idea, and I have given examples of its success for people of college age. That is much too late for the great mass of people caught in the poverty cycle, because most of them will not be prepared even to enter college because of inadequate preparation throughout childhood. I continued to think about the problem after retiring from the university, and was unhappy that I would not be in a position to continue working on such an important need. By great good fortune, an opportunity appeared for me to move toward the goal of a better education throughout childhood.

After I retired from my administrative duties at the university, I received a visit from biochemistry professor Joseph A. Walder, who wanted to discuss my long-standing interest in early childhood education as reflected in the *Opportunity at Iowa* program. We had appeared together on a panel before talented high school students two years earlier, and he remembered my comments about the need for an early start in education. After more than two decades of reaching out to younger and younger children, I had concluded that even the preschool years were too late for many children whose families were caught in the vicious cycle of low income, inadequate education, and lack of employment skills. The development of such children is further hampered by low expectations from their families as well as the society in which they live, and the disastrous consequences of the destructive behavior that is associated with alienation and absence of hope. Walder had a long record of support for low-income and minority students, and offered to provide seed money for me to develop the ideas distilled from my life experience. He had already established the Foundation for Advanced Studies as a source of money to develop ideas emanating from professional activities in the university, which he proposed to use as a funding source. I welcomed the opportunity, and spent the next several weeks to develop a blueprint for the Institute for Learning and Development (ILD) to support the families of children from the prenatal years through high school.

The programs of the institute were designed for *all* children with no restrictions based on family income or ethnic identity. Although special attention would be devoted to children most at risk, the quality of the programs should be attractive to families at higher as well as lower income levels. Financial support would come primarily from the families and local businesses, with capital development assistance from public and private community agencies and federal sources. Scholarships for low-income families would be offered by the institute to supplement funds from many other sources, primarily at the local level.

The institute provided for four interrelated programs. Mary-Care Centers would provide healthful nurturing for infants and outreach to expectant mothers so that conditions such as malnutrition and drug abuse that adversely affect the development of the fetus could be corrected. Early Learning Schools were modeled on the most effective existing preschools, with the Iowa City Montessori as an example. After-School Programs were developed to supplement regular elementary-school education by using the facilities of the schools or other community agencies as centers for children in grades one through seven or eight, where the older ones can "tutor" the younger ones under the guidance of a trained supervisor. Higher Learning Programs for students in grades nine through twelve were designed to improve retention and academic achievement, provide experience in the work world, and funnel badly needed money into the pockets of low-income families.

ILD programs were not based on the assumption that low income per se is a tragedy or even an embarrassment. Adequate food, clothing, shelter, and health care for every person is a valid goal, but it was recognized that the pursuit of material wealth far beyond those necessities is not a basic element of some value systems. Honesty, living in dignity, resolving conflicts without the use of violence, and demonstrating concern for the welfare of others are valued more highly, and such value systems deserve respect. ILD programs assumed only that a low family income should not be an inescapable trap for children, and they were designed to prepare each person, especially the young, for opportunities to pursue his or her individual goals. The ILD program document states that its goal is "A cure, not a palliative — the 'have-nots' should learn 'to fish' and thereby become independent and prosper for a lifetime rather than living from day to day on the 'fish' of public welfare."

ILD was able to assist a few community agencies in Iowa City and Davenport, but lack of funds has virtually halted its work. Some of the ideas are reflected in the Neighborhood Centers in Iowa City, and the Montessori school has been able to realize some of its goals of better space, better-prepared teachers, and scholarships for children from lower-income families. I still believe in the proposed programs, and hope that they can be implemented on a national scale. My dream for the Institute for Learning and Development is an unfinished chapter in my life.

Thoughts while Thinking

After traveling to dozens of the major cities of the world, staying in many first-class hotels, touring on luxury cruise ships and trains, and enjoying some of the world's finest cuisine, I still like beans and greens.

Wyrick, about vegetarianism: "If animals are not to be eaten, why are they made of meat?"

Little daughter of a Ph.D.: "Oh yes, daddy's a doctor, but not the kind that does people any good."

Proud husbandman: "She ain't much fer purty, but she's hell fer strong."

Tourist, regarding the Louvre: "It's magnificent — I could have spent the entire morning there!"

"Success has a thousand parents, failure is an orphan." Anon.

An insatiable appetite for property is the dynamo of capitalism; a lack of concern for those with the least control over their lives is its Achilles' heel.

Words on a shingle in Amana: "Too soon oldt, too late schmardt."

Economics places greed on a mathematical basis. No wonder it's the dismal science, and no wonder politicians love it.

INDEX

SINGULAR LIVES

The Anti-Warrior: A Memoir
By Milt Felsen

Black Eagle Child: The Facepaint Narratives
By Ray A. Young Bear

China Dreams: Growing Up Jewish in Tientsin
By Isabelle Maynard

Flight Dreams: A Life in the Midwestern Landscape
By Lisa Knopp

Fly in the Buttermilk: The Life Story of Cecil Reed
By Cecil A. Reed with Priscilla Donovan

In My Father's Study
By Ben Orlove

In Search of Susanna
By Suzanne L. Bunkers

Journey into Personhood
By Ruth Cameron Webb

Letters from Togo
By Susan Blake

My Iowa Journey: The Life Story of the University of Iowa's
First African American Professor
By Philip G. Hubbard